Find Work

Worth Doing

JASON MUTZFELD

DEDICATION

For Dirk-

May you do work that makes the world a better place
and find it is work worth doing.

Table of Contents

Foreword 1

Preface 3

Section 1: Understanding Career Management........................ 5

Dream Jobs..6

Why you should take responsibility for your career. 18

Why do you need a career strategy? 20

Why you need to think like a career coach.................................22

Why you need career engagement..25

Why you should always be 'Reinventing Relevance' 28

Section 2: Career Misconceptions 32

Correcting Career Misconceptions..33

Career Misconception #1: "I just need a job, any job." 37

Career Misconception #2: "I should love my job" 40

Career Misconception #3 "Job hunting should be easy"..............42

Career Misconception #4 "My skills are my most valuable asset"
....44

Career Misconception #5 "Your education defines your career
destiny"...46

Career Misconception #6 "A good job is a secure job" 49

Career Misconception #7 "There is a secret key to success"........51

Career Misconception #8: "Work should make you happy" 54

Career Misconception #9: "Don't quit a good job".....................57

Career Misconception #10 "Follow Your Passion" 59

Reconception: A New Model of Work...63

Section 3: Finding Your Career Character *65*

Your Character M.A.P **66**

M.A.P Question #1 "What Do You Want?" **72**

M.A.P. Question #2 "What Can You Do for Others?" **78**

M.A.P. Question 3: "What Can You Do?" **83**

M.A.P. Question #4 "What Have You Done?" **87**

M.A.P. Question #5 "What Are You Doing to Make This Happen?" **92**

Strategy = Adding it all up **95**

Section 4: Career Tactics – Writing Your Resume *97*

Embracing the 'Next Normal' **98**

What is a resume anyway? **99**

There is no 'I' in 'resume' (resume-speak) **101**

Resume pitfalls **102**

Hallmarks of a good resume **104**

Resumes show Accomplishments **105**

Resume keywords **107**

How a resume is read **109**

Technical considerations **110**

Contents of resume **115**

Writing Activity #1 - Getting Started **116**

Writing Activity #2 - Resume Header **120**

Writing Activity #3 - Summary & Accomplishments **124**

Writing Activity #4 - Work History **127**

Writing Activity #5 - Supporting Information **131**

Writing Activity #6 - Finalizing your document........................136

Cover Letters..139

Dealing with Applicant Tracking Systems (ATS).....................144

Section 5: Career Tactics - Job Search..*148*

Misunderstandings about the job search.................................149

Your PCI - Personal Career Inventory 151

Planning your search...153

Your social media plan 155

Online job search...161

Keywords...166

A word on 'hidden' jobs and networking.................................167

Section 6: Career Tactics – Interviewing *170*

How to ace the interview 171

Preparation phase 172

Interview questions you may encounter 175

The S.T.A.R. Method..178

Interview locations 180

Informational Interviews and Career Fairs 182

More interview types..183

Questions you need to ask 184

Closing the interview & effective follow-up.............................186

Appendix A: Resume Information Checklist *189*

Appendix B: Sample Resume *190*

Appendix C: Cover Letter Sample...*192*

Appendix D: Resume Action Words List.....................................*193*

Foreword

In 2012, my boss barred me from interviewing a candidate because she wasn't pretty enough. "Beauty's in the eye of the beholder," he said, "and I just don't see it in her." Angry, devastated, and stunned I went home that night and told my husband what happened. "Don't go back," Jason said, "You can't work for someone who doesn't share your values." A few days later, I resigned (giving more than adequate notice) without any idea what I would do next.

The weeks that followed led us to brainstorm many ideas. Together, we founded Merrfeld Career Management, a firm dedicated to guiding people through their careers and building up their confidence. From the very moment we set foot upon this path, Jason became a tireless advocate for people who were looking to reinvent their careers, build upon their passions, and do work worth doing. His passion excited people and his love for new ideas shined through in everything we did.

Let's be honest, in the beginning, we had no idea what we were doing but Jason's quiet confidence never wavered. Deep down he knew that we could make a difference in people's lives by helping them pursue work that fulfilled their unique passion and personal mission. His love of theatre, passion for learning, and steadfast belief that everyone is entitled to a career that matters to them led to this book.

"Fix what's right with you," was adopted as our company motto based on the idea that the good in each person outweighs the bad and that by strengthening what you do well you can build opportunities you never thought possible. It marries up nicely with Jason's personal mission statement, "Do work worth doing," one that he's built upon for himself and others throughout his career.

Like many of us, he found himself at a professional crossroads. The work he loved was no longer fulfilling and the industry had transformed into something he no longer wanted to be a part of. Never afraid of diving deep for personal reflection, Jason began to explore what it meant to reinvent his relevance. He began to explore alternatives that had only been whispers in the back of his mind before. At the time, I don't know that he understood the impact or magnitude this work would have on so many.

His efforts to reinvent himself began to be noticed by colleagues, peers, and clients. The pages of this book are filled with the very steps he walked to create work worth doing. From defining his purpose and mission to the tactical steps of writing a resume and employing a job search strategy, Jason takes you step-by-step through the process. His ability to explain the meaning and purpose behind each step will guide you through why these things are so important and how to apply them.

I believe there's nothing more powerful than the knowledge to build a fulfilling career. Jason does an excellent job of providing this vital knowledge and breaking down the steps to reinvent your relevance and find the work worth doing. What sets him apart is that he's been there and done that. He's employed these very strategies, experienced the uncertainty and imposter syndrome, and moved forward to build a successful career defined by his own value system. He's faced scrutiny and judgement as we all have but he's never let that stop him. Instead, he's turned that into fuel that drives him to equip others and write this book.

If you find yourself without the passion or drive you once had for your work it might be time for a change. Equipping yourself with the tools and knowledge to reinvent your relevance – to define work worth doing, is a valuable investment of your time. Jason guides you through the process and helps you build the strategy for the next steps with empathy, clarity, and kindness because he's been there too.

-Michelle Merritt

Managing Partner, Merrfeld Career Management

Preface

It's a common question that is rarely, if ever, spoken out loud:

How the heck do you figure this career stuff out??!!

Handling your career may seem like a huge undertaking and it often is! Don't panic though because we're going to walk through it together in this book.

We will start with an introduction to the philosophy and practice of what is called Career Management. From this overview, you will gain a fresh perspective on how careers function and how you can use the same methods career coaches use to enhance and advance your work.

The next section lays the foundation to examine what's not working in the present world of work and what holds back your career performance and hinders growth. We won't just tear down without building up though. We will propose some alternative mental models that we have found work well for our clients and that you can use to architect a new attitude towards your working life.

The third section is about uncovering the mental narratives we all use when setting a strategic vision to leads us forward. We will examine ourselves and how we find meaning in our work by looking at our personal character, specifically how we motivate ourselves through Mission, Attitude, and Purpose. These three items serve not just a guide for goal setting but will also keep you on track as you progress.

The final section presents the tools to help you act on your strategic vision. We're going to give you the nuts and bolts of what the career management process is by sharing the tactics we use to write resumes, set goals, search for a job, and other insights that will keep you moving forward. Any strategy that doesn't have action is a dead one.

If you are currently at a career crossroads, remember that the answer to this unspoken question is that the answer is already inside you.

You just have to choose to listen to yourself and make plans accordingly.

Ready to get started?

Then let's go!

Section 1: Understanding Career Management

"Far and away the best prize that life has to offer is the chance to work hard at work worth doing."

—Theodore Roosevelt

Dream Jobs

When you were a child, there's a chance you were asked "What do you want to be when you grow up?" You might have said "An astronaut!" or any number of fantastic dream career choices (pro athlete, musical superstar, CEO, movie star, etc.)

Adults don't always listen to what children say they want to be when they grow up because children, being children, are notoriously fickle. Children also don't understand how the world actually works. They're stuck in a world of fantasy and dreams. Adults generally respond with a "good for you" and go on about their day. It's simply small talk to the adult. To the child though, it is more than that. Dreams are the things that make childhood so much fun. Infinite possibilities and choices bounded only by the imagination.

If you asked a teenager "What are you going to do for the rest of your life?" and they responded with "Become an astronaut", you're faced with more options on how to respond.

You could respond:

"Good for you!" and go on about your day. Small talk.

"Interesting, how are you going to make that happen?" Interest that might start them thinking of the real-world implications, assuming they hadn't already.

"That's next to impossible, what are you really going to do?" This is just being a kind of a jerk though, isn't it?

Now when we ask our adult selves "what do you want to do with your life?" we almost always go straight to option 3 and go full-on dream crusher jerk-mode. We discount our own dreams, hopes, and vision.

Why?

Because being an adult and facing that question we have several issues to deal with that children don't. We have responsibilities. There are bills to be paid and mouths to feed, even if it's just our own. The sacrifice to follow a dream involves a lot of work, risk, and only a possible chance of achieving our intended reward. When we imagine dreams, they're safe, when we pursue them, we have skin in the game and can suffer a loss if we don't play the game properly.

Ultimately though all of those responsibilities can be dealt with up to a point. There's an even greater constraint that adulthood has to deal with. When you make a choice to follow a dream, you take responsibility for making it happen and you have to defend that choice to others. We could be laughed at- I think that's the worst fear of all.

Shortly after I completed my undergrad in communications and theatre, I ran into the father of a high school friend. He was a draftsman, a well-paid working-class skilled profession back in the day. He asked me "So you got your theatre degree? How'd that work out for you? I see you're not on Broadway".

Ouch.

(For the record I never wanted to go to Broadway, I wanted to join Second City then teach, but still.)

I was humiliated. Had I let my family and myself down by thinking I could teach theatre and speech? It shook me. I abandoned that dream and took a safer route into the computer field. I had run screaming at the first sight of a battle. Folded up like a cheap card table. Not my best moment but it took a long time for me to ever get back. Everywhere I looked I saw the same thing- people afraid to dream. Just like me, somebody had asked then "when are you going to give up on your stupid dreams and get realistic".

I had, as so many people do, to come to the conclusion that dreams were apparently for children. Apparently wanting to do something was a sick joke that only adults understood. Maturity was knowing that there was no Santa Claus but humoring kids who thought there was.

Have you felt that way too?

I have some good news then.

The good news is that this denial of what we want and the demand that we sacrifice it on the altar of what is practical is, in a word, hogwash. You're supposed to dream! To say you don't is to deny what you feel and want which divorces you from a part of yourself. It's detrimental to your own peace of mind not to dream.

Let's take a look at how dreams for 'grownups' work.

This is the life of anyone in the Career Management field: A client wants help to achieve their career and life goals and sometimes they may seem improbable, if not downright impossible. Let's go back to our astronaut example. Being an astronaut is a tough job with a tough list of job requirements.

To even be considered, NASA requires the following at a minimum:

1. U.S. Citizen
2. Master's degree in a STEM field from an accredited school
3. 2-year professional experience of 1,000+ hours pilot experience
4. Able to pass the NASA physical
5. Demonstrated skill in leadership, communication, and teamwork

All that said, is it impossible to become an astronaut? No, a very select group of people become astronauts every year. Is it probable you can become one? Meh, probably not. It is highly unlikely that just anyone will be chosen and trained to go into space. This is why when you want to become an astronaut, it's important to start early. An adult may foster in a child a love of space through encouraging this dream. If it's something they lose interest in, no big deal. Childhood is about exploring different options. A teenage astronaut wannabe might be presented with the requirements to get into space so they can start putting in the work sooner rather than later. Time is on their side but it's fading. If the child and the teen are the same person then you've gotten a rare gem of a personality that knows very early what fires them up. When they become an adult and they're still on that track they've trained and prepared as best they can to go for it. Sadly, we know that even with early intervention and constant investment of effort and time, things don't always work out to plan. Life gets in the way and even 110% effort can result in an outcome that says "sorry, no".

So, did you miss your shot to go into space (or whatever dream) because of your childhood choices? Should you have paid better attention? Is it all over?

No, it's not over, just different.

I have met many people who lament what might have been if they had chosen another path when younger. We cannot change the choices and decisions we make in our youth. We often mistake the well-intended advice that "the choices you make today impact your future" as a dire warning that translates to "you only get one shot at happiness, so if you screw it up now you'll miss out on it forever!" This lack of nuance haunts many adults.

One thing I've learned working with college students over the years is that inexperienced people make lousy career counselors. This doesn't stop us from forcing teens and young adults to make career choices without actually giving them any training on how to do that. If we did, we'd spend more time in their education focusing on what it is that makes them original and what drives and excites them. Instead, it's a quick fix of 'this is what you need to know' and out they go into the workforce. We cannot blame the educational system though, 'know thyself' has been the foundation of wisdom since the dawn of Western civilization. It's up to the individual human being to get things figured out. Your teachers can't do that for you, nor do you want them to (honest, you don't). Some people don't ever figure it out.

To make matters worse, some people take issue with even the word 'dream'. Some are concrete thinkers who believe we're talking childhood fantasy or literal nighttime sleep illusions. Some also look at the world as the unjust, unfair, and unpredictable ball of happenstance it seems to be and use this as grounds to dismiss dreams as being not worth the effort. I argue not that these opinions are wrong, I argue instead that they're missing a larger point. A dream is not just a goal or ambition, but instead a reason why we do something.

So are we out of luck if we gave up our childhood dreams? Are we done for if we missed our shot? How do we find our dreams as adults? It starts by reevaluating the value of dreams in human life. The value of the dream is found in the pursuit, not the achievement. A dream moves us forward by firing us up from within. motivating us through inspiration and potential. It is not something outside us, it is a part of us. Stop looking for a 'Dream Job' and start looking for the dream in the job you're doing.

How do you find 'the dream in your job'? To start this process of redefining your dreams in career terms, I coach people through a process called 'Reinventing Relevance'. We focus on finding those things in ourselves that drive us, inspire us, and enable us so we can see what we can make out of our lives. Relevance is important for anyone in the job market, you need to be the right answer to the right question for the right person. That is what grounds you to the adult reality you find yourself in. Reinvention implies something else though. It implies you've done something before and now you want to do something else. You 'invented' your career and ultimately yourself through a process of experimentation, risk-taking, and effort that has produced the person you are today. Reinvention is the art of embracing change and alternating your trajectory to become another type of person or do another type of thing. The person who reinvents their relevance best learns what about themselves is right, not wrong, and focuses their energy into things that advance them in the direction they need to go. That could be a promotion, a new role, a new career, an entirely new vocation- the sky is the limit. Reinventing your career means finding your dreams again starting where you are today.

One of my heroes is Walt Disney. I'm not alone in idolizing him as he had such an impact on 20th century American culture while he was alive and well past his death. Look at the legions of Disney fans and you'll find people whose lives are touched to this day by what he achieved. He was far from perfect and much has been said about his bad habits and personal faults. As a hero to me though, he was what a hero should be- he was inspiring. Inspiration comes from the

Latin 'inspirare' meaning to breathe. Inspiration is literally the breath of life. Without it, we would die. Literally in Latin, figuratively in English. Dreams are supposed to inspire us to take action and through that action find happiness and satisfaction. The heroic journeys which are undertaken in the stories Walt told, and his namesake studios continue to tell, almost always begin with a central character taking responsibility for a transformation they're challenged to make.

Walt was a good example of what happens when you take responsibility for following your dreams from where you are. It's an oft-told tale of a young Walt taking a train ride back from New York after learning his intellectual property was no longer his and he was about to be on the verge of bankruptcy. Again. He recalled a little mouse that used to visit him late at night at his animator's desk in Kansas City and was inspired to create Mickey Mouse. The rest, as they say, is history.

Well, not really. Walt was a lousy artist, he relied on his righthand man Ub Iwerks to draw the character. His wife Lillian came up with the name Mickey. It was a collaborative effort. What Walt brought to the project were Mickey's spirit and (literal) voice. Walt wasn't just a storyteller- he was an actor. Not that he read other people's lines but that he had the uncanny ability by all accounts to make a flat storyboard come to life through his telling of the tale presented on it. He said of himself that he was like a bee, buzzing around his studio pollinating ideas in people's heads. His legacy is undeniable because he continues to inspire countless multitudes to put a little Disney magic into their lives. The parks that bear his name contain placards commemorating their opening day and explain in no uncertain terms that these places serve not just as somewhere to escape reality to become enthralled in wonder and charges guests to take back some of what they've experienced into the cold world beyond the boundaries of the parks. So too do the films that bear his names energize audiences of all ages to challenge the darkness and bring out their own light to drive it back. Lofty words to describe a simple concept: Dreams are the responsibility of the dreamer to make real.

Dreams are in some ways, magic. I visited Walt Disney World in Florida a few times with my parents as a child. I was in awe of the wonderous things I saw and vowed that I would, somehow, take that magic home with me. I spent many days designing attractions and parks in my basement as if I was a junior Imagineer. As I became an adult though, I long forgot a lot of what had inspired me until the year I started grad school. I had a milestone birthday that year and my wife knew that between work and school I was going to be under a heavy load, so she arranged for us to take a trip to Walt Disney World. I was against it at first, because I felt it was extravagant and a waste of resources to indulge in a vacation like that. She insisted saying that we needed to go. Thankfully, as so often is the case, my wife was right, and I was wrong. I came away with a new question: What is special about the 'magic' I experienced there? Could that be found in everyday life?

I toiled on this question through most of the grad school and it became the topic of many papers and class discussions- how can you get people to have a magical experience that transforms them? Slowly, as I began to study more and more about how human performance and engagement work the answer became obvious. The way to transform people is through inspiration which gives hope for a better life. Hope for a 'great big beautiful tomorrow' as Disney fans call it. This wasn't about engendering false optimism or toxic positivity but about how to put real 'meat on the bone'. Hope was the thing that drove back the darkness and if you wanted people to have hope you had to get them to believe beyond the material and move into the realm of the imagination. You have to make dreams not just tangible but attainable. What kind of world would we have if everyone looked beyond the dreary shadows of the apathy to see a world they actually wanted and were willing to work for? I think that would be a grand step to making a better world. So, what does it take to make that inspiration tangible?

Effort (and lots of it). Dreams take sacrifice to become tangible. That is where they become precious to the dreamer.

A dream is not merely a wish. We wish for miracles and hitting the lottery despite the mathematics not being in our favor. The major problem some people have with dreams is they don't always come true. That doesn't mean we shouldn't work for them. What's the alternative- spend time just doing 'stuff' waiting for life to be over? This is the default setting in the game of life for most people, unfortunately. "Give up your goals, get a job, get old, then hopefully die peacefully with as little pain as possible."

Ugh.

This is why so many people give up on their dreams. They compartmentalize the things they're interested in and instead choose to work at a job that may not excite them. It's considered the mature thing to do. Not cynical or negative, but prudent and sensible. Labels applied to justify not trying to understand what fires them up and settling for being useful, more specifically employable, in somebody else's estimation. The opinion they might have about the value of their work or their hopes for the future never seems to enter into the equation. It doesn't have to be that way. You still have to be employable and prudent for sure, but when you bring your whole and original self to the table, you'll find that it's not only good for you but it's also good for your job. You will perform at a higher level than you ever imagined. A dream is not a wish, it's what guides your choices.

The role of choice in your career is something that most people think is only for teenagers and college students. They're the ones with all the time and the least amount of burdens in life (until those loans kick in). Adults have to be practical and realistic and not worry about chasing dreams, right? The fact of the matter is that adults chase dreams every day. They work to build a life that creates an ideal outcome. They strive and toil to make it happen. They just do it for somebody else. Generally, the dreams they follow are those of their employer. Rarely do they even consider what they might want to do. As an adult, you're on a path that you don't always choose because you have responsibilities and people who count on you. This is why people dream of striking it rich and becoming fabulously wealthy- they think it will bring options that bring freedom. They want a fresh start, a do-over, a magical 'reset life' switch. Except much like becoming an astronaut at 35, it will probably never happen. I hear you saying now "Great! So what can I do?"

It starts by taking your dreams and determining what it is that inspires you to follow them. Career coaches often start by going back to the original question because even to adults there is much to be learned from the answer. The problem many adults have with the question "What do you want to do?" is that is often mistaken to mean there is only one linear path to the end goal. From a concrete thinker's perspective, if you want to be an astronaut, you train to be an astronaut, then become one. You can substitute any high-profile dream job for an astronaut- fashion model, rock star, pro athlete, even 'fashion rock astronaut'. Training A leads to Job A.

The mistake isn't in the question, but the interpretation. Instead of thinking of dreams as goals with clear paths, think instead of them as ideas we want to express and share. Go beyond personality to performance- not who you are but what you can do or want to do from where you are right now. If "what do you want to be?" means "what job title or position do you want to have?" it is very limited. To a child, it makes sense though- it's how they interpret the world. People are teachers, firefighters, janitors, etc. They think in terms of roles and titles. If you try to explain to a child what a full-stack web developer or currency trader does, it will most likely be simplified down to "you work with computers" or "you work with money" and go no further. My father was a journeyman electrical technician at an automotive parts plant in the town I grew up in. In kindergarten, we were asked to draw what our parents did. I drew my father in his blue work shirt holding a wrench because I had no idea at age 5 what an electrician did! I suppose if he ever used a wrench to fix a high voltage machine press then something wasn't right.

If I had been a career management coach in Kindergarten (which would have been weird), I would have gone to what does my dad actually 'do' instead of "what is an electrician?" I would have drawn lightning bolts on wires and he would have wire snips or a multimeter. In high school, when I actually took electronics and science classes, I learned even more about what he did. It sounded sorta cool. Instead of learning how to wire up machines though, I combined it with another passion I had as a youth. I wanted to be a Disney Imagineer because I saw through their designs a wonderous future of technology and engineering. Studying Electronics and science led me to digital technology, specifically computers. As a child born at the dawn of the Digital Age, I was the first digital native in this strange new world. But I had a problem on my path to becoming an engineer - I was really bad a mathematics. I found that I was really good with computer troubleshooting and systems though. I spent decades jockeying bits and bytes across networks and herding cats through a burning building at times. The dreams of Imagineering never really left me though, and it carried over how I approached service management and dealing with users. I could not be an engineer, Imagineer, or programmer but I did what I could. When I discovered that all my years of dealing with people combined with my ability to tell stories and educate others in a unique. The dreams of my childhood never died. It did however change. That's how dreams survive- they adapt.

I was not an electronics technician like my father was and I wanted to be when I was young. I became a different kind of technician and later a technology guru. All because I watched my father do his job, which he loved. It almost killed him at least once- multiple amps severely burned him and damaged his heart. But he still went to work as long as they would let him. He had responsibilities certainly, but it was more than that for him. He liked what he did. Most important, he set an example for his youngest son. He said, "Listen, I don't want you to work for somebody else breaking your back, I want you to work with your brains and enjoy what you do". My parents and aunt sacrificed to make sure I had a computer and I would go to college. They wanted me to not just make them proud though, it was about me doing something that I loved doing.

Long after my parents passed away, I came to a plateau in my career trajectory. I had a choice to make, should I stay doing what I was doing, or pivot into something else. I had bought into the default settings of life, which is brought defined as the attitude of 'it doesn't matter if you enjoy it, just do it and shut up'. I wanted to find out how to best use my talents to build a life and career around the dreams I had as a kid. A better world. Helping people find joy. But was afraid. That fear was sensibility, a lack of confidence, and a host of other adult excuses for putting off making life changes.

A very nasty car accident gave me the wakeup call I needed. It triggered an early existential crisis that convicted me if I would not die in a cube; I would have to make a drastic change. I used my research and analysis background to rip apart the career systems in the modern world. The idea that there is one great and perfect job for you is a myth. In the search, I did find my next career destination which was far removed from where I had been. I found myself dealing with a human problem that seems to slowly kill more and more people each day: doing work that doesn't matter. This problem and the mission to solve it became the dream in my job.

What I found when I peeled apart all the layers of cultural meaning we apply to work and our jobs was that it all distilled down to this:

You're investing time and effort into creating something.

That something can be as simple as a paycheck or as complex as the foundations of a meaningful life. You have a responsibility for what you're creating.

You also have to ask yourself – is all this effort worth anything? Do you love what you're doing?

As I broke things down, it became clear that it is the choice of the individual to assign as much meaning to their job as they desire. It's also a responsibility, because once you know that it is up to you to assign purpose, mission, and attitude to your work you cannot simply ignore that responsibility without paying a hefty price in anger, bitterness, and regret. Imagine you'd truly always wanted to go to space and that dream was denied you. Depending on your history that pain may be all too real. I've got to imagine that potential astronauts stuck on the ground, gazing up at the stars, are not happy people. Perhaps you already are paying that price. I would suggest that the reason is you've been trained year after year to just go with the flow without ever stopping to realize you could try to steer the ship.

I get it, it's rough. You have a million reasons why you have to stay doing what you're doing. I did too, believe me. Wanting something different seems scary and risky, but with plans and systems to guide you, you can slowly, incrementally change the way you're working.

Even if nothing changes, you can at least change yourself. You can find work outside of a job even. The important thing is to try. Dreams, visions, goals, whatever you want to call them at the end of the day don't become real without effort.

I became a career coach because I saw a definite gap that I believed needed addressed. Most professionals like myself who work with youth and those who work with adults are focused on finding employment. I'm all for both of those things, but as I taught those I mentored over the years: Being employable is more important than merely being employed. Your character makes you employable because it shows not just that you're a skilled person but that you have a vision. You have a dream. How you work is a vital part of human life and t defines you in many ways. You spend much of your waking adult life at work. Feeding your soul matters as much as feeding your body.

Over the next few chapters, we're going to take a look at some of the internal resources you'll need to get started on your career journey. These are the foundations you'll need to sort out before you head out on the road towards creating your dream.

Why you should take responsibility for your career.

In 1995, Microsoft introduced a new feature to its dramatic overhaul of the Windows interface. It was a menu button on the toolbar. To get people to notice it they didn't just give it an icon or name it 'menu' they tried something novel.

They labeled the button "Start".

Start was an apt metaphor to use to name the button because it was not just descriptive, but also functional. It told you what to do – Start (here).

Life certainly has a starting point. At one point you're not here, then you are. You begin by being alive. It couldn't be much simpler than that. From there you begin a rapid succession of firsts and 'starts' that got you going into adulthood. More often than not, you were told where and when to start. When you reached adulthood, however, those instructions stopped for the most part.

Your boss might disagree. Bosses are great for telling people when to start and stop. They think it makes the world go around. They are somewhat right in that, mainly because we aren't taught when we're younger to do much else besides waiting around for someone in charge to tell us to do this, do that, etc. We're trained at an early age to obey. A lot of folks get wise to this trained obedience and rebel. Sadly, this too goes awry in that this self-boss mode can be functionally anti-social and at odds with getting anything done. It seems that both obedience and rebellion can gum up the works.

So what can we do about this? Is there a way forward?

Let's consider that there might be a middle ground between blind obedience and blind rebellion. I believe that the middle ground is found in taking responsibility.

Consider how people work in groups. Organizations are built on systems of activity that, through metrics and supervision, keep things humming along like a machine. They are designed to reduce uncertainty and risk as much as possible with rules and procedures. If organizations were machines with 100% automation, then you'd have no problems. People are independent thinkers and there's no way to enforce 100% compliance or mitigate 100% of the risk of individuals doing things outside of required parameters. Organizations are forced to rely on individual responsibility to make positive choices. Have you ever worked at a place where you had a lot of autonomy and empowerment? They're generally happy places to work because people are treated with respect and trust. The opposite type of organization isn't built on that level of goodwill but instead relies on paranoia and suspicion. By and large, those are toxic workplaces that have a high turnover. Business, in general, can sometimes seem like it's weighted heavily into the paranoid camp, and playing fair seems to be for chumps and losers.

As individuals, if we assume higher levels of responsibility for our actions we are judged favorably by others. That level of responsibility has to encompass ourselves as well, meaning we cannot assume responsibility for everything. Some things are just out of our control. We can take responsibility for our responses to things that happen, our choices, and our actions as much as reasonably possible. If we obey a rule, that's on us. If we disregard it, that too is on us. Sometimes, we don't even get a chance to decide how we respond. Regardless, the results are on us.

What does that have to do with your career?

The answer is 'Everything.'

Responsibility is what makes a job or career into something that brings out the best in you. You don't need someone to bring it out of you or show you how to do it. You already know. You have to admit that to yourself and respond to that part of yourself that wants to do more than just survive. Humans want and need to thrive.

The field of Career Management is how we can uncover and design our personalized guide and use it to advance our vocational goals.

Why do you need a career strategy?

Career Management is an afterthought to most people. It shouldn't be, but let's be honest- it's not usually given much consideration. Career Management is usually lumped in with the business concept of self-management, sadly another afterthought to most people.

Perhaps you're thinking to yourself "Spare me the high-minded mumbo jumbo about vision, cut the crap and tell me what to do!" Hopefully, you're not. If you are let me address why this is the wrong approach to take when thinking about your career. There is just one word to describe it: "shortsighted".

Most of our adult lives are spent in the pursuit of making a living. Given that fact, how you approach the way you work can be a defining expression of a person's beliefs and principles in society. Careers have become so central to modern life that there is a dangerous potential that they can be given too much importance and tip over into extremes of workaholism. When work never ends or toxic careerism drives what defines success then everyone, not just the employee, has a problem. In the United States, individuals rarely hesitate to tell people what they do when they're asked. People outside the United States consider it a strange, if not rude, question because to them our culture is driven by a work ethic that places the earning of a paycheck as the sole definition of who we are as a person. More often than not, they are sadly right. Maybe it's because of our lack of social cohesion or lauding of the rugged self-made individual in our mythos that we do this. Regardless of the source, it's not helping.

Some don't buy into this and think of jobs, careers, vocations, professions, whatever you want to call it as simply a means to an end. An ability to pay the bills and maybe buy some nice things along the way. They get a job and then are expected to do it just well enough to be left alone and not bothered about it. It's a linear process – apply for work, get work, work-work-work, try not to get fired or at least get better work before they do fire you. Employers even seem to want to be in on this game. For all the talk of leadership, engagement, and culture very little is done to improve the workplace. Little thought is given to the enjoyment of work or if the work has any meaning to it. This is a huge social problem because people are not able to thrive in an environment where they are just parts of a machine.

Let's not waste this opportunity. Managing your career is even more important in the present age of digital transformation and economic disruption. Your career should not just be an afterthought but be should an investment that will support you and your family. In the Industrial Age, you did what you were told and only worked as hard as you had to. Those days are gone. There are many employers that exploit this new reality of job insecurity to their advantage. This is also a reason to take responsibility for and manage your career. If you don't want to be under the thumb of a boss you hate, having a plan to not only avoid this sort of situation or fight back when it happens is vital to your economic survival.

Having a strategy to get the results you want want and need in the world of work is no longer an option in the 21st century. Why do you need a personal strategy? Because you want to have a say in how your life goes, not just resign yourself to following the herd (potentially over a cliff). A strategy is what makes your visions and goals a reality because it tells you what actions to take and where to direct your attention.

Why you need to think like a career coach

In business, you frequently will find managers, leaders, and coaches. Sometimes these three roles are played by the same people. Regardless of how many people are involved, you need all three roles to achieve success because all three help people produce results through better performance.

- Managers ensure systems run as they should to get the optimal result.
- Leaders set goals that the systems are designed to produce.
- Coaches focus on removing the obstacles that prevent people from performing to the best of their abilities because it is the people in the end who make all systems work.

In terms of your career, you can think of yourself as a business of one. Your job is a system and you manage it to get the optimal result. You set vision, goals, and strategy for your career that dictate what your job is supposed to do for you. Coaching your career should be what separates a ho-hum job from a career of distinction and excellence.

People generally think of two models when they think of coaching. Neither is wrong, but neither is a full representation of the field either. The first is a sports coach, whistle in hand, sending players up and down the field of play. The second is the life coach, which helps you with the personal problems you have that you don't need a full therapist to solve. Career Coaching is not about scoring the most goals or solving your life issues. Career Coaching is about solving your work-related issues. It's worthy of the focus to ensure that we perform in the workplace so that it doesn't impact the other parts of our lives. Working well is ultimately about our well-being as a whole. A healthy attitude about work can help you keep it in its proper place so you do not succumb to some of the toxic habits that destroy us slowly from within (workaholism, careerism, toxic managers, soul-crushing industries, meaningless jobs, etc).

Every coach will tell you that they're not in the business of telling people what to do, they're in the business of analyzing performance and bringing out the best in people. Career Management is about finding what parts of work aren't producing the results needed so you can work around them by focusing on the parts that are. Don Clifton, one of the leaders of the Positive Psychology movement, and Peter Drucker, who is considered the father of modern management theory, both referred to this focus on developing talents as strengths. Strengths are those parts of ourselves that, when we invest in them, develop into assets that are undeniably valuable in the world of work. These assets are the foundation for improved performance and by focusing on what's right with you instead of what's wrong, you'll find that your improved confidence and other professional skills are noticed by others.

It goes without saying that the future is made from the events of today and today is made from the events of the past. Naturally, when you analyze human performance, it's helpful to have some context of what's come before so you can chart what you desire to come next. In order to build a better philosophy of work, we have to start with where we've been as a collective group. It's the background from which we approach the idea of working so it's the key to understanding what has a positive impact on us and what has a negative one.

How does coaching work in practical terms though? It can vary from coach to coach, but usually, the process breaks down something like this:

1. First, you have to start by defining what you're trying to accomplish.
2. Ensure the fundamentals of good performance required are covered and understood.
3. Then move on to taking a baseline, listening, and observing what goes on and what the resulting outcomes are.
4. Analyze these outcomes in relation to what's being done and see if the outcomes being asked for are in alignment with what's happening.
5. Craft a plan to change behaviors to improve alignment that includes metrics to measure compliance.

6.   Monitor ongoing behavior in relation to outcomes and make adjustments accordingly.

7.   If outcomes are determined to be unobtainable or no longer the best investment of effort, define a new goal then create a plan to pivot in that direction.

This is why coaching is different from just management or leadership. Coaching is adaptative and improvisational, not giving answers to solve problems but helping those solving the problem ask the right questions to find the answers on their own. You can also apply these coaching practices to yourself through self-assessment. That's what we're going to work through in this book- we're going to walk you through exercises designed to get you looking at yourself in a new way. When you're finished you will not only see things more clearly, but you'll be more confident in your ability to create your meaningful work.

Why you need career engagement

My mother was fond of the phrase "Make yourself useful". Frequently she began a request with "Make yourself useful and…" Above all else, my mother possessed a strong work ethic and she worked hard to instill it in me. Like most people though I never considered that a work ethic was something that applied to anything other than your paying job or work/vocation. In actuality, your work ethic influences everything you do because it is how you choose to make yourself employable (or 'useful') to others.

The simplest definition of employment is that we're talking about the trading of time and skill for a paycheck. It's the model that has existed from before the Industrial Age and will serve us for a while longer as we go into the Information Age. It's taken as a given this exchange of goods and services is the foundation of employment. When you dig into this model though you see there's an incentive issue. The incentive isn't to do the best work for the most amount of money. It is to do the least and lowest effort work for the amount of money. Any sense of pride comes from the individual, rarely from outside motivation. When you're inspired and encouraged to do better work, everyone benefits. That benefit doesn't always translate to rewards, however. That's why strategy is important in Career Management- you not only feel the rewards of a job well done, you need to see those rewards as well.

In the industrial economy of the mid-20th century, the coveted position that most people aspired to was that of wearing "golden handcuffs". That was the metaphor for job security were the handcuffs that restrained you to your job were financial, not physical. Your lifestyle required you to stay put in order to enjoy the safety and benefits that your job provided you. You were locked in and had less freedom but like farming before it, there was a sense of certainty about the arrangement. This sense of security was prized above all, even if though was illusionary, and sometimes used to control an employee's options. Our early-21st century information economy has a different set of rules, job security is still sought by many but granted to an extreme few. The difference now is that the security, while still coveted, is known to be an illusion.

We live in an economic reality where the asset that is you is defined by the value you bring and how relevant it is to your employer or client. The most valuable human resource isn't technical skills or education, but instead, it's the personal assets that exist in the individual because each individual isn't just a replaceable cog or widget but a fractal microcosm of the organization as a whole. Customer service, sales, culture development, troubleshooting, security, and all the main functions of an enterprise are performed not by carefully designed systems and metrics but by human beings. There are human traits that cannot be automated. Organizations now value 'engagement' as a metric to determine if their employees are truly committed to what's going on.

What is engagement though? There are many definitions, but you can simply answer the question "Do you care?" to determine if you're engaged.

Don't care? Not engaged.

Do care? Engaged!

Engagement, the act of not just paying attention but giving a damn about what you're doing, is what drives people to move to do more than is asked of them. It is the drive in your brain, guts, and heart that fuels you and rewards you for a hard job well done. When was the last time you felt like that? Finding that inner drive is the difference between people whose work is not only outstanding but in demand. It's a unique advantage that's in short supply. Finding out how you engage can help you uncover not just where you perform better but also potentially untapped talents and skills.

Like most things in life though, the question comes down to "what's in it for me?" No ideal motivates better than one that is win-win. Nobody wants to be a martyr to the cause of their work. What you can gain by tapping into your personal engagement style is a sense of enthusiasm and inspiration. Business isn't always fond of human imagination, ingenuity, and innovation if it doesn't add to their bottom line. That's to be expected because much like people they have motivations and goals that drive their efforts. The individual should not be expected to surrender their sense of self or drive to achieve in service of their employers' goals, though sadly that is all too often the expectation. Knowing what drives you, what you're good at, and what you're trying to do is important to maintain your sense of self-worth and self-respect. Due to economic pressures, we can give it all up too easily for expediency's sake.

As you take responsibility for your own personal economic enterprise called your career you will hopefully be coached or coach yourself to compromise where needed but also hold fast to what you're trying to do. That's what will drive your performance, keep you engaged, and provide you with a sense of satisfaction. Those traits alone will place you in a category that very few people will ever obtain. This isn't just about you though; it is about the greater good because this is something we should want for everyone. By building your professional character in this way, you commit to and model behavior that inspires others. Working in this way is truly doing work worth doing. Go the extra mile to be engaged by giving a damn. If you don't, then move on.

Why you should always be 'Reinventing Relevance'

There's a lot of waste in the world. We waste food, effort, money, energy, time. Sometimes this waste is shameful. Other times it's unavoidable and not really anyone's fault. It can be hard to differentiate. There is one thing that we can waste that is almost universally regretted in the long term- wasting a wake-up call. Sometimes we waste them because they're subtle but the ones that grab your attention are the ones that remind you of the universal constant of human existence. Your life will end one day and there's nothing you can do about that.

Thanks to an incorrectly timed traffic light and a distracted SUV driver I was fortunate enough to receive a wakeup call on my way to work one day. I walked away with a totaled car, a few bruises, and a renewed awareness that human life is finite and that as I entered middle age it was only going to get even more finite with each passing birthday. I sat down and made a plan, looking at where I was at present and where I wanted to be. I defined what my mission was, what sort of attitude I was bringing to my employer and then set goals to achieve to give me a sense of purpose. This renewed meaning was to be my guiding star as I moved into the second half of my working life.

One of the cornerstones was looking at my career in higher education technology management and re-evaluating where I stood. I was trained up in my undergrad in Communications and Theatre with a hefty minor in History at one of the few remaining small liberal arts colleges in the Midwest. My graduation coincided with the dawn of the World Wide Web and I subsequently applied my learning skills to master technology and create a thriving career in I.T. Ultimately my background in training, commitment to education, and love of learning led me to move into Educational Technology focused on distance learning. Shortly after my accident, I began to study for my graduate degree in Learning Design and Technology from a notable university with a focus on Human Performance. I graduated with a near 4.0 GPA and completed the course entirely at a distance. Shortly after obtaining my degree, my boss called me into his office to discuss "my future". I, needless to say, was excited. I had lobbied for years that we need to better align our department to the needs of both our instructors and students. I had almost begged for the chance to work with students and faculty more, often being told to focus instead on other more pressing concerns. My patience was going to be rewarded though.

Well, sorta. My boss kicked off the meeting with a question. "Are you looking for a new job?" I was shocked by this, but I understood why he might have thought that. I responded no, I was more than happy enough where I was. His response was to ask why I'd not gotten a degree in technology then. I did, I replied – Educational Technology is what we do. I'd been clear this was where I was wanting to go. I wanted to advance. I wanted to teach. I was committed to staying where I was and in the same department, but I was interested in aligning what I did to better suit what I was good at and wanted to do. I was told I was too valuable where I was to consider any changes. It was a soul-crushing experience. My entire career seemed to have been brought to a dead end. I was expected to give up. What I wasn't clear at the time was this was something beyond my bosses' level and beyond his boss all the way up to the very top- there was nothing that could be done to alter my position or place in the hierarchy because it was not a strategic priority. The system wasn't able to adapt to my needs because it wasn't designed to do that. Sometimes development is like that- it's not part of the system. That's not anyone's fault, it's a design flaw but one that we have to deal with. I would bring it up a few times more, but eventually, the message was clear- if I wanted to move up, I needed to move on. I was responsible for my job advancement, so the choice was clear.

Unlike some who find themselves in this predicament, I had options beyond just finding another job. I gave an admittedly half-hearted attempt to find different yet similar work all the while ignoring two facts that were staring me in the face: I already had another job I loved and I hated the one I had. This might give you pause but sometimes obvious answers aren't always evident to the person with the problem. This is why coaches are so valuable. My wife had gone out independently as a career coach many years prior and the business had grown into a full business, not just freelancing. I worked part-time building content and coaching clients to find their strengths and career talents but worked full time to provide things like health insurance and steady income. The business had grown enough to provide a full-time income for us both. I loved to coach people because they, to me, were the ultimate platform to impact the world. Each person was part of a larger social whole and helping them find the satisfaction and joy of work worth doing impacted so many people beyond just my own sphere of influence.

I was also tired of doing what I was doing. I had, like so many, stumbled my way into the path I was on and was feeling trapped by my 20-year old self who made the choice to pursue it. After spending half of my life in technology I found that moving to the field of helping people was within my grasp. Naturally, there was a lot of fear, doubt, and uncertainty that had to be overcome plus a large dose of planning. I had to learn to listen to my intuition and internal cues, letting them give me the feedback that I used to make the choice to break free. Was it hard? It certainly was! There were a lot of hurdles to overcome but nothing was stopping me other than myself. I was able to self-coach and be coached to overcome my inner negative voices though. The leap of faith into entrepreneurship and professional independence was worth it looking back on it though and I would do it all again.

Months later I was meeting with my business coach on our strategic plan for the year and we were working on how to define what career coaching actually produces for people. After much back and forth, the idea of 'Reinventing Relevance' was born. It not only summed up what I had done in my own career switch but it was the best metaphor for what we did for career seekers, career changers, and advancers. Your career success is defined by your relevance and it needs constant innovation to stay vibrant and alive. It is what every person with a job is responsible for to themselves and their employer - being and staying relevant.

What is 'relevance' in this case though? Relevance is a cornerstone of communication – if your message isn't relevant to the person you're trying to reach, they won't hear it because they don't think it is important. Secondly, it's a state of value. A plumber isn't relevant to you on a day to day basis. If your toilet backs up and you have it spilling out onto the floor, a plumber is extremely relevant to your immediate need. Fire insurance is relevant to your home although you don't always know it until it burns down. Relevance is being a valuable asset, not just an afterthought.

'Reinvention' is taking something and making it more. This is what a career change is always about- taking what you have and making something else (location, title, function, etc.) with what you have. It is something that has to be constantly pursued because relevance can fade if you get complacent. Combining the drive to reinvent yourself with an eye to staying relevant can make all the difference in a career change.

Ultimately, reinventing relevance is about more than finding a new job or a new employer. It is about finding your own voice. As a coach this is my job, not to merely tell clients the answers or direct them in the right path but to help them have the 'aha!" moment that shows them they had the answer all along. In the movie The King's Speech, King George VI is pressed by his speech therapist to the point he loses his temper and exclaims "I HAVE A VOICE!" You show up every day in how you work and it should be a reflection of your unique abilities and attributes. The best way to express that is to be relevant, a valuable and valued asset, in everything you do by constantly working to stay that way. Your career path is alive but it won't stay that way unless you constantly attend to it. Have the courage to change what doesn't work.

Section 2: Career Misconceptions

"I did then what I knew how to do.

Now that I know better,

I do better."

- Maya Angelou

Correcting Career Misconceptions

Time for a quick pop-quiz!

1. Your doctor tells you that you have a viral infection. You ask them for an antibiotic to treat it and they refuse to prescribe it. Is your doctor doing the right thing?
2. You pull into a gas station and they're completely out of gasoline. You have a gasoline car. Do you put diesel fuel into your tank instead?
3. Somebody gives you a US two-dollar bill. You've never seen one before- are they giving a fake bill?

Answers:

1. Yes, antibiotics can't kill viruses
2. No, you'll ruin your engine
3. No, while they are rare a $2 bill is a real denomination of US currency

These questions are absurdly easy if you're an adult. If you asked these questions to a child, they might not pass as easily because they don't know any better. In a child's mind they might believe that pills from doctors cure things, fuel is fuel, and they may have never seen a $2 note before.

Think back to the last time you learned a new fact- did it excite you just a little? Perhaps it even frightened you a little? A common occurrence of this kind of revelation is to find out you've been using a word incorrectly for years. Pronouncing espresso as 'eX-presso' for instance. Even if you continue to keep saying it the old way, you know you're doing it incorrectly going forward. Once a fact is learned it's very hard to unlearn it!Did you know there's a hidden arrow in the FedEx logo? If not, look between the second 'e' and the 'x'. See it? If you didn't know it was there before, you'll no longer be able to NOT see it. This is a form of mental awakening. A mind stretched with a new thought will never go back into its original shape. New ideas can change your thoughts and, by extension, your actions. This is what social 'awareness' campaigns are all about. The same is true for marketing- make impressions to make a sale.

The marvelous thing about the human brain is that it never stops learning. If you examine how the brain processes information you will see that the brain processes feedback of all kinds and adapts behavior based on previous experience. Human existence is a constant process of learning, unlearning, and re-learning. Learning is the foundation of all human endeavors.

Think about how you get a job. Where did you learn to get a job? In school? From your parents? You might not even know; you may have just picked up this skill along the way. It is something most people just seemingly know how to do. You have preconceived notions, essentially thinking shortcuts, that guide you through the process.

From a career management standpoint, this can be a problem. Career Management is assisting the individual to make plans to ensure the employment they apply effort to pays off for them in ways they want. If you just 'go with the flow' without designing a plan to make that happen, you have to take what you can get. That's the default setting of the job market – take what you can get when you get it. Don't plan, don't dream, don't complain but simply 'shut up and do your job'.

Why is this an issue? Because you spend a large portion of your adult life at work, so if you don't choose a career path or job wisely you can find yourself doing work that tears you down in the long term instead of building you up. Humans can certainly work with default settings because we've been doing it for thousands of years. For the majority of the planet, default is the best they can do. There is no shame in that- all work is virtuous if it's done for the right reasons. If you think about your older relatives, chances are good they toiled in jobs they really did not enjoy because it was what was available to them at the time. This was considered normal and you didn't have to like your job. You just had to do it. This was and is still a burden that many, if not most, adults have to face every day. Work takes up long stretches of time and it's not worth the effort beyond the fact that it is what pays the bills. It's a sad and bitter truth, but a truth, nevertheless.

I grew up in a working-class family in a working-class town where two philosophies seemed to be used by parents to explain the world to their kids. One, which seemed to be the majority, was "don't get above your raising". This philosophy taught that life was tough and your life wasn't going to be any better than your parents had it. Take what you get and hang in until you die. The second, which I was fortunately blessed to be brought up believing was "Do your best and try to be more than you come from". In this philosophy, life was tough, but you had to put your energy into being better and doing better. Your gift was the ability to make things happen and you should find something that excited you. Do that because life is short. Don't take your life for granted or let the fear of failure hold you back.

For those who do have career options, there is a level of ethical peril that comes into play. If a person has been gifted, through chance or endeavor, the ability to choose how they spend their time, they have a responsibility to not waste that gift and show gratitude by making sure that the work they engage in is worthy. This means making choices and those who have the privilege of options about what kind of work to do have a responsibility to choose as wisely as they can.

To make a wise choice, you not only have to be willing to think about the problem, but you also have to work from the mental framework you have. If you have outdated knowledge about a topic, you will make choices based on outdated information. Making mistakes is part of the process and it is important for learning. That doesn't mean we should not try to work from an always up-to-date set of facts. Misconceptions are general ideas that are based on faulty or outdated notions. They aren't lies that are disproven with fact, they are generally merely ideas that are out of date and no longer a good guide to base your thinking on. Much like a road map from the 1940s, you'll find that while the actual geography has not changed much but the roads are almost completely different. Career decisions are often made on misconceptions because career guidance is often built on economic, commercial, and organizational ideas that are no longer relevant in the modern-day. You can however correct those misconceptions by replacing them with newer mental models to guide your decision making. In essence, you need a new map.

If life is learning, unlearning, and re-learning then the next chapters in this book fall into the unlearning/relearning category. We're going to examine 10 less-than-accurate ideas that I frequently encounter working with clients. My job is to coach you here, not to teach you facts. Why? Because being skeptical is also part of the learning process. You will examine each statement and then I'll offer you an alternative to consider. The choice is up to you to take them and make them your own guide. Or you can also disregard them. I believe that you'll find the alternative suggestions work well for you.

Ready? Let's start deconstructing some career misconceptions.

Career Misconception #1: "I just need a job, any job."

What does it mean:

A job is just a means to an end. It doesn't matter what you do, just as long as it pays. You could dig ditches, flip burgers, or whatever – you're just out to make money.

The true parts:

All work has dignity if it's done with pride and it betters others. No position, no matter how "lowly" should ever be used to judge a person's character or status if it's an honest job. More often than not, having a job (bad, good, or indifferent) is preferred to not having a job at all.

The philosophical underpinnings:

This reflects a very Materialistic view of economics. Materialism is sometimes lumped in with greed and acquisition but that's not a fair judgment. Materialism is a philosophy that says this factual, material world is all that is and gives no attention to how you feel about it. When talking about science or hard data that is a true statement because facts don't care what your opinion is, they're still facts. However, when you're dealing with people there is something that can be overlooked: how people feel.

Why it doesn't always work:

Yes, that's right – emotions matter. Now if you're squirming in your seat reading that I can assure you you're not alone. Jobs are an extension of the business process and, with very few exceptions, emotions are considered an almost forbidden topic. Business doesn't care about your feelings, so they don't belong in the workplace- right? No, actually they do belong there. Why? Because you're a human being and even if you're a master of compartmentalizing your emotions you cannot deny they exist. Think of all the resources and money spent to numb them into a quiet state- staggering amounts of cash are spent to beat them into a bloody pulp that you can sweep under a mental rug.

How you feel about a job that takes up your precious time, develops you as a person, and requires your attention, matters. Here's a breakdown:

1. Your time and attention are valuable because they're limited.
2. The time you spend at work develops your skills and knowledge, so you should receive a return on your investment.
3. If you don't care about what you are doing or, worse yet, are actively annoyed by what you're doing you won't do it well. This reflects poorly on your character.
4. If you don't work in a job that suits your talents and temperament, you will not be able to do a good job even with extensive effort.
5. You will resent your boss. You will resent yourself. That's not healthy.

So, how do you feel about your present line of work?

Suggested Replacement:

"Make your work matter"

Stephen Covey in his book 'The 7 Habits of Highly Effective People' listed Habit #2 as "Begin with the End in Mind". Before you do anything, look at it and decide if the intended actions move you towards your targets or goals. Sound advice for sure.

Perhaps take it a step further though and make that endpoint not just the end of the day, project, or job and look at the end of your life. That's right skip to the last page so to speak and consider your final thoughts. One of the most frequent regrets of people who are dying is that they didn't spend time doing what they want to in life. They only did what they were told they could do. Sorry to be a downer here, but it's an important question we should ask ourselves frequently because it's a good metric to determine the worthiness of what we're doing.

So even if you have to take a job that's just what you need to get by, are you going to settle for just what comes along or continue to try to find something that works better for yourself? Wayne Dyer used to say, "Don't die with your music still within you" and it's a haunting, yet necessary, thought that few will ever entertain. Instead of taking just any job, consider instead doing work worth doing – work that has meaning and matters to you and to others.

Work worth doing might be just earning a paycheck to support your family and if that's your motivation hold onto it and be proud of it. If that is pursuing a dream, be proud that you take the risks. If you're like most people you trend a middle path of pursuing what you want while earning a living doing things that don't always excite you. Take pride in that as well. Just promise yourself you'll never settle for "just a job" and stay there- it's a recipe for a life you might regret in the long term.

Career Misconception #2: "I should love my job"

What does it mean:

This can be taken in two ways. One way is the premise that you should love what you do which is internal to yourself. Another is to love your actual role or position, which is obviously external to yourself. In either example, the idea of having emotional commitment is important.

The true parts:

People can love abstract concepts, but when you talk about the action of demonstrating love then this is usually a personal connection. The word is overused for certain "I love you guys!" "I love the Indianapolis Colts!" "I love this ice cream!" When you mean it in a serious manner, you're expressing a desire to display commitment, loyalty, trust, and a host of other pro-social and positive virtues through your actions. In that sense, you bring love with you to your job.

The philosophical underpinnings:

The idea has been around for a long time and for our purposes we're tracing it back to the notion "Love what you do and you'll never work a day in your life". If you do it out of love, you'll not mind the expenditure of blood, sweat, and tears.

Why it doesn't always work:

In your career, you will have many jobs and positions. Some will be horrible, some will be wonderful, most will be a combination of those two things. 'Love' can complicate both the good and bad aspects of the job.

One hazard comes when you try to overlook the bad parts, even when they hurt you, because of your love for the job. This is far more common than most admit! The problem here is that you'll often stay in a place that is not a good fit for you or, worse yet, actively causes you harm.

Another is forcing yourself to love something you don't doesn't make sense either because forced emotions require tremendous energy to maintain and that energy could be used elsewhere. 'Fake it until you make it' is often repeated like a mantra is modern workplaces but if you never end up actually making it then all you're doing is faking. Fake love isn't love, it's a lie you're telling yourself and others.

Finally, you can love your job too much. You can get attached to something that, if it happens to disappear as jobs and positions tend to do, can lead you into a state of immense grief and loss. The bitterness of rejection that comes from being let go or not getting what you in the workplace want eats away at you. Some employers can leverage your love of the job over you and use it to convince you to work for less than you're worth.

Suggested Replacement:

"Enjoy your work"

Love is a powerful emotion and using it for everything, including your job, can cheapen its value. Instead of loving your job, perhaps commit to enjoying it instead?

When you break down the origin of 'enjoy' it means 'bring joy', which would be the alternative I would propose. If you bring joy and enjoy your work then you not only are a better person to work with, you remove some of the 'normal' misery that a workday can bring. You also free yourself, and your work, from having to give you joy because your source of enjoyment comes from inside you and not just from your job. Enjoyment in the workplace is an attitude we can choose to develop. It's also a good metric to determine if you should stay or leave a job. Enjoy your work by bringing joy to your work.

Career Misconception #3 "Job hunting should be easy"

What does it mean:

Looking at it linearly, job hunting is fairly straight forward. Find an open job, apply for the job, interview for the job, get the job. What else do we do in life that looks like this when examined at such a high level? Dating springs to mind. Find a single person, talk to a single person, date person, fall in love.

Holding this idea that getting a job should be easy is based on a deceptively simple premise: If the steps can be explained simply, it's a simple task. Holding this opinion asks a job seeker why they are struggling and then blames them for it. They can be assumed to be either not smart or lazy to fail at this "simple" task.

The true parts:

This works partly because, at this extremely unrefined level, it is actually pretty simple. At this level even brain surgery is simple. Some take it further to frame it in their own experience and think that just because it was easy for them to find a job, it is also easy for everyone. The truth is evident to them because it was true in one instance. Life is rarely this simple.

The philosophical underpinnings:

This idea is frequently found in the educational system. Degrees, alumni status, certifications, licenses often promise that once you've obtained "it" then people will seek you out without you even having to try to look for a job. "It's like shooting fish in a barrel, you'll always hit one!" This isn't to say this doesn't happen, just that it's rare. These stories of 'jobs were so easy to get they were handing them out' are frequently told by the same sort of folks who walked uphill both ways to school through 3 feet of snow for 20 miles each way. Whenever somebody says 'do this and it will be guaranteed to work' chances are they're trying to sell you something. Your mileage may vary, so be skeptical and be smart.

FIND WORK WORTH DOING

Why it doesn't always work:

It doesn't work because you don't actually want it to work. That's not some kind of subconscious 'fear of success' nonsense, it's an actual fact- you do not want it to be easy. Well, at least too easy. Nothing worth doing is generally easy, because we are wired as a species to overcome difficulties and face challenges. If something comes easy to us, we frequently don't hold it in high regard.

Suggested Replacement:

"Be eager to do hard things."

It's said that "life begins at the end of your comfort zone". By doing things that stretch our abilities we grow as individuals. We can also find both pleasure and satisfaction in doing hard things and those are byproducts of hard work that are frequently overlooked in favor of finding a shortcut. Don't miss the opportunity to enjoy the process because you didn't want to put in the hours and effort. You'll thank yourself that you did.

Career Misconception #4 "My skills are my most valuable asset"

What does it mean:

"Skills" covers a host of different items in the career seeker's arsenal. It can include hard skills such as technical skills or the so-called 'soft skills' (I prefer the term 'professional skills') such as leadership. It can also be shorthand for experience and demonstrated competence. Essentially anything you would list on a resume as a personal attribute could classify as a skill.

The true parts:

You can't ignore the role of personal attributes and skills in the job search process. That's just how things are. You have to be able to do something to get a job.

The philosophical underpinnings:

This goes back to the Industrial Age of employment and since industrial production is still a major factor in the world economy it has stuck around. An employee was hired to perform a function in a system that they were responsible for. Even before then, journeymen from trade guilds would engage in their "trade". You exchanged your services for money. You still do- it's how modern employment works. As a philosophy of work, it's not going to change any time soon, if ever. Even employees in the Digital Age Information Economy have skills that employers pay money for.

Where this model goes askew is that is it doesn't go far enough. At a basic level, a person contracts with another to perform a skilled service. At this level, the individual is merely a replaceable part in the system. People can be regarded as widgets or cogs, which greatly undersells the human ability to do good work. Most employers don't ask much of the individual other than to show up and do what they are told. The ability to go beyond your functional duties isn't always accounted for.

Why it doesn't always work:

Where this comes into play for the individual is in the first stages of the job search process, specifically your resume. Your resume will never get you a job. Why? Because that's not its purpose. Your resume is what they call in sales a 'line card' – a line of services you offer for a price. The 'what gets you a job' is actually a 'who gets you a job'. That 'who' is you.

The issue is that it implies your value as a potential employee is self-evident. This isn't to say that it can't be, but that is only seen in job markets where open positions are plentiful and the particular skills you have are in such high demand that anybody (sometimes any literal 'body') can fill the position if they have the required details. A skills value is always as self-evident as a job seeker thinks, either. To truly make the case for their value and relevance, a job seeker has to make the case for them.

Suggested Replacement:

"Showcase your ability to get results"

To perform work that goes beyond you checking the required skills on a list of attributes to one that suits your personal needs means you have to actually engage in the sales process. This might turn you off if you have a negative view of the sales profession, however, you're already engaged in this process just by being in the job market. What is job seeking if it's not sales? Find a prospective client (employer), solicit business by submitting a proposal and supporting marketing materials (cover letter and resume), then meet with them to listen to their needs (interview) and provide potential solutions (that would be you).

This idea also elevates your skills to showcase them as the solutions to a problem, not just a commodity to trade for cash. You are a business of one and you can consider your employer as your partner or client, not just another taskmaster barking orders. This is a model that may not change the world of work in the grand design of things but adopting it as your personal approach might just change your attitude towards work itself.

Career Misconception #5 "Your education defines your career destiny"

What does it mean:

The concept is that your degree, or lack of one, is your career destiny. It also applies to your major or specialization- do you have the 'right' one for the job? What about certification? The ability to show that you can learn and develop yourself is important in the job market and it should not be overlooked.

The true parts:

Having a college degree does make the job search easier and functions a social proof a person is educated to a certain level of knowledge and skill. Not having one or having the 'wrong' degree, 'wrong' major', or being from the 'wrong' school make things much more difficult.

The philosophical underpinnings:

To understand this one, you have to know a little bit about how degrees are perceived in the business culture. It was once explained to me like this: "obtaining a college degree is proof to an employer you can eat a BS sandwich for 4 years and get something from it". I don't endorse this notion but there is a basic nugget of truth in it. A person with a degree, whether it was obtained 4 years after high school or earned as a working adult should be justly proud of achieving their degree. Even the act of completing high school is challenging and should not be undersold.

But the ultimate failure of this idea is rooted in a human social bias we all fall prey to at one time or another. It is the bias of status- the belief that certain cultural attributes or social proofs place a person in a special class above the rest. To put it more succinctly: people regard college degrees as something important because the person with the degree is of higher 'quality'. That can be unconscious or conscious, but the outcome is the same. Because this bias fails to judge a person on their character, background, quality of education, or abilities but instead on the possession of a piece of paper then it is socially unfair. The presence or absence or degree is not an excuse to offer a free pass in the job market. If you wouldn't want somebody to do that to you, it stands to reason you shouldn't do it to someone else.

Why it doesn't always work:

[This one gets on my nerves so if I sound like I'm on a soapbox, please excuse me.]

Here's a question: if you had to get vocational advice would you go to somebody who's 18 and ask them what you should do? Why do we expect those same high school and college-age people to make career decisions and then stick to them, sometimes for the rest of their lives? Much is said about getting into the 'right' school and getting the 'right' degree that the message of what college and vocational education is supposed to be about is lost. On top of that, the debt load creates a situation that limits economic choices in the future. The ultimate insult? Most places that require a degree don't even background check to determine if you actually have the degree you say you have. If it's required for a licensed or professional position, they most likely will, but for all the rest it's not always something the hiring manager even considers doing.

Degree, degree type, lack of a degree, etc. is used as an excuse by employers to hire or not hire. Sometimes they actually believe you do need them, sometimes they don't. Educational degrees are a crapshoot- they may open doors and they may not. It's a game nobody seems to be able to win.

Suggested Replacement:

"Show that you can learn"

Despite what you may think from the preceding rant, I actually support the idea of education. I happen to have an advanced degree in education which is how and why I got into coaching. While much is said of education, very little is said of what value it can acutely bring beyond the obtaining of a degree or certificate. That piece of paper is just an indication that a person is educated but speaks little to their actual character as a learner. The ability to learn, unlearn, and relearn is the hallmark of adaptability and employability.

Training is just instruction, but learning is shown through behavior. Lifelong learning will make you employable far beyond mere instruction or training.

As higher education continues to evolve we may well move past the elitist nature of credentialism, but for now, the best thing we can do is change our own personal attitudes towards them. They're not a badge of honor, they're a responsibility to show up as an educated person who can demonstrate learning.

Career Misconception #6 "A good job is a secure job"

What does it mean:

This is a statement on the quality of a position that is built on how stable it is in terms of economic volatility. A good job is frequently seen as one that pays well enough, pays consistently, where the work is consistent, and provides certain other benefits. A good job is something most parents wish for their children to find. Steady, reliable employment.

The true parts:

Security, specifically consistently being paid for the work you do, is a good thing to have. It is hard to conceive of anyone who wouldn't like that level of reassurance that despite things that go on in the world you'll still be able to pay the bills. Even entrepreneurs who build businesses and artists who work gig-to-gig will frequently confess that steady income and benefits would be fantastic to have.

The philosophical underpinnings:

This notion is a cornerstone of what is called the American Dream. The premise of this idea is that individuals get paid well and work is consistent, allowing them to afford the comforts of life and that consumption is what drives the economy. This is also found in Fordism, the business dogma of Henry Ford – pay your workers well and they'll be loyal. Having spent time in the Industrial Heartland of the Great Lakes, automotive industry workers would refer to their jobs as 'Golden Handcuffs' – you were locked into a job that was steady and stable. They never stopped to think that they were still in handcuffs, regardless of their metallic content.

Why it doesn't always work:

There is a term that you may have heard before called 'Security Theater'. It is frequently used to describe the process you go through at the airport before you board a plane. There are rituals and procedures you must endure to ensure that your flight will be a safe one. However, upon examination, there is little evidence that the process actually provides the safety it's supposed to guarantee. Job security, for the most part, is also a form of theatrics. You might be promised that if you do a job well you'll be taken care of but the hard reality is that you could be let go at any time for almost any reason. You're not even guaranteed that you'll be able to receive unemployment if you are let go. Job Security is a myth, and that means good jobs aren't secure.

So what is a good job then if it's not secure?

Suggested Replacement:

"A good job is an investment"

Instead of judging the value of a job by security or pay, consider taking a big picture view. If you consider the impact of what you do in the present on your strategy for the future, then it makes sense to shift focus to the time spent in a position as an investment. Look beyond the paycheck to the development opportunities and experience you gain during your time at the job. The value of the job then becomes what you get out of it long term as it impacts your greatest financial asset- your own employable skills and talents.

People will spend time at a job they don't like because it's considered 'secure' when they instead could be spending time doing things that build up their future.

Career Misconception #7 "There is a secret key to success"

What does it mean:

There is "something" that separates successful people from normal people and that 'thing' is confidence...

...or maybe it's optimism...

...perhaps it is hard work...(??)

Regardless, there is a surefire, never-miss 'trick' to becoming a successful person and you will always fail to achieve success until you find it, unlock it, and make it your own!!

...At least that's what is said shortly before you scroll far enough for the webpage to display the link to buy the course/seminar/class that will teach you this magic 'secret'.

The true parts:

Successfully achieving a goal isn't easy and you need to have certain attitudes to achieve it. You do have to be confident, strategic, optimistic, etc. as you are pursuing your desired result. Success is not always handed over to just anyone, it is earned. You have to work for it but hard work alone is no guarantee. You need luck and serendipity which are easier to find when you have the right point of view.

The philosophical underpinnings:

There is a Latin proverb "Audentes Fortuna Iuvat" which translates to 'Fortune favors the bold'. It has stood the test of time because it is usually true- boldness does help you achieve your goals. Fortune is not just a stand-in for 'luck' but rather an actual goddess named Fortuna who was the goddess of lucky breaks. For much of human history, people have sought divine favor to ensure that outcomes break their way and our misconception plays into that. The person making the statement has a shortcut, much like a divine gift, that they want to bestow upon you to help you out. It might be a relative, a friend, or a stranger that is offering you this advice to make your journey easier. We almost always tend to jump at the chance for this 'secret' knowledge because the human brain is wired to find shortcuts to make its job of processing feedback easier. The ultimate mental shortcut is to avoid thinking about tangible action but rely on mantras, charms, and other magic formulas to make things happen.

Why it doesn't always work:

The good news is there is no magic that you're missing out on.

There's another proverb that impacts anyone trying to reach the next level of any career: 'Anything worth having takes sacrifice'. While there are short cuts to be found, they rarely replace the need to rely on internal resources such as hard work, dedication, discipline, and resilience. You have to give (sacrifice) effort and resources to make a dream become real. Otherwise, you might not be satisfied with it.

If there was a real secret to success it would be that there is no secret! Success is open to anyone who wants to work hard enough and is willing to keep trying until they make the luck that they need. Because 'success' is an idea that differs from person to person only individuals can define what it is, hence, there can be no universal answer for everyone.

Suggested Replacement:

"Make your own luck"

Resisting the allure of shortcuts and get-results-easy schemes is difficult at times, but not impossible. For anyone managing their career, it is vital to understand that achieving goals is never certain, but that with the properly timed actions you can tip the odds in your favor.

The best thing you can do when starting out to achieve any goal is to not compare your journey to anyone else's. We are surrounded by people for whom success (seemingly) came easy and those who had to take extra steps. Sometimes we see people cheat to win and sometimes we see people cheated out of what they were rightly due. Comparing ourselves and where we are doesn't help you, it only holds you back. Maybe it's true your cousin has gone from intern to VP in 5 years and you've never had a promotion your entire career.

Should you curse the fates, Fortune, or the Universe that you've not had the same things happen to you? You certainly can, but it won't do you any good and will probably make you feel worse! Celebrate those who succeed and get back to what you're doing. Keep trying, adjust your strategy as needed, alter your goals as necessary, just don't stop trying to be the best that you can possibly be.

Luck is just taking opportunities as they come and making the best of them. It's not something bestowed by supernatural forces as a reward for effort, it's merely playing the cards you have been dealt the best way you can. Being a 'success' is not a title or honor bestowed on you by society. Success is whatever you choose it to be and it is totally subjective. The best way to be a success is to take pride in whatever you're doing to make things happen in your career and thanking your 'lucky stars' you are doing what you can.

Career Misconception #8: "Work should make you happy"

What does it mean:

If you had supportive parents as a child and you told them your career plans "I want to be a musician" they might have responded, "Whatever you want, so long as you're happy". When you make a choice, your friends might say "Well, as long as you're happy with it". To wish somebody happiness in that sense is to say effectively saying, "Good luck" with a possible subtext of "you're going to need it".

When you say it yourself as a declarative statement, you're saying that your intended outcome is to feel a state of happiness. When you're talking about careers or the workplace, the statement is frequently "I'm not happy at work" which implies the inverse "I should be happy at work". Managers will ask their staff "Are you happy here?" Happiness in the modern American workplace is seen to be a requirement.

The true parts:

Happiness actually is important in your job and workplace. If you never happy at work or you derive no happiness from what you do then chances are you need to move on, because you're not going to do as good a job as somebody who does exhibit the positive emotions we commonly label happiness. Happiness shows you and others that you care about what you're doing and are engaged in your work. It's also important for your co-workers because consistent negativity can be a real drain on team morale.

The philosophical underpinnings:

This is really a no-brainer in many ways. Happiness is a positive, pro-social emotion and if you asked most people if they'd prefer to be happy or sad, your money should be on the majority opinion being in favor of happiness. Jobs and the workplace, where adults spend the majority of their waking hours, weren't always considered a place where emotions like happiness mattered. Jobs are an economic function in the old school approach to business and were studied rationally with little regard for satisfaction or engagement in the workforce. As you study motivation through a behavioral lens you will find that productivity, customer experience, resilience, psychology safety, and other human factors that dramatically impact the bottom line are improved when positive psychological principles are the focus instead of a materialistic approach to management.

Why it doesn't always work:

That said, should we just put all our efforts into promoting our happiness in the workplace? Sadly, it won't work because happiness isn't something you can pursue directly. Happiness is a byproduct of each individual's taste, temperament, and talent meaning you can't take a direct, one-size-fits-all approach to manufacture it. No job will be guaranteed to make you happy. The human brain engages in a process called Hedonic Adaption meaning you might be happy in the short term as your brain receives a boost from the neurochemical cocktail that is happiness, but eventually you'll return to a general state.

Suggested Replacement:

"Happiness comes from meaningful work."

Work will never 'make' you happy because that's not how happiness works. So, what can we do? One suggestion is to focus on doing things that produce happiness in your life, so your happiness is not dependent on external factors such as a job. Imagine if you had the best job in the world and you were happy every day, but then you were fired. Where would you find your happiness? Your happiness is something you need to cultivate internally, not just expect it to magically come to you because of some external source.

Abraham Lincoln once said, "People are usually about as happy as they make up their minds to be". Instead of trying to find happiness, try to focus on doing work that produces meaning for you, and then you can focus on that which helps you produce happiness. If that's your job, then embrace it and be grateful you have found it! If your job doesn't make you happy, then understand that it's okay to feel that way. In both cases make up your mind to find out what drives your happiness and bring that happiness with you into the workday. You'll find a workload that was once intolerably heavy was a little lighter. Don't stop pursuing happiness, just know that it comes from within you and not outside you.

Career Misconception #9: "Don't quit a good job"

What does it mean:

What if you don't care to move on, or up, at your current job? Is there any reason to think about career management when all you desire is to stay where you are? This statement recognizes that not everyone's ambitions are to constantly climb a metaphorical career ladder. There is romantic nostalgia for things that don't change. There's also no reason to believe bigger, faster, or novel is automatically better.

The true parts:

Consistency is an effective strategy that builds a career a person can be proud of. As long as the person isn't avoiding something by staying put there's not much harm as long the employment continues to be steady and rewarding.

The philosophical underpinnings:

This is essentially a risk management strategy similar to investing regularly and then letting your nest egg continue to compound. If there is no outward pressure to move on, why would you?

Why it doesn't always work:

Imagine working your entire life at the same job – going to the same place, day after day, eating lunch, going home, and then repeating the next day. For some, there is no need to imagine it because they live it. Now imagine that you're close to retirement age and, out of the blue, you job is declared unnecessary and you're out of work. Much like a wild animal that has lived its life with humans, the survival instinct was never developed and the person who thought they were safe is suddenly facing a grave crisis – a need to start over, having never learned how to adapt.

Tragic? Certainly, it's a heartbreaking tale that's all too common. You may not want to move on from your current job, but your job may have other plans for you. There's nothing as constant in life as change.

Suggested Replacement:

"Always be ready to change your work"

The Scout Motto of 'Be Prepared' is what you need here. When is the best time to update your resume and check in on your professional network? Yesterday. When is the second-best time? Today. The worst time – tomorrow, because it may never come! Being ready to move onto another job by keeping your skills sharp and expanding your contacts and spending time to develop yourself is always time well spent. You never know when the need to reinvent your relevance in the workplace is going to hit, so be ready for it by embracing change – you'll be able to turn disaster into an opportunity if you play your cards right.

Career Misconception #10 "Follow Your Passion"

What does it mean:

Sometimes you'll see this on inspirational merchandise and it's frequently given out as advice by people who have already achieved a level of success. The principle behind it is that you'll be truly motivated to achieve great things if you feel a strong emotional desire that draws you toward the goal.

The true parts:

Desiring something strongly is an effective motivator. On the most basic level, the drive to survive motivates us to seek food, water, air, and other essentials to keep us alive. An old adage "You have to be hungry for it" means to truly show that you're ambitious you have to want your goal like it is necessary for you to survive. This metaphor sticks around because it is relatable.

It has been said that if you have a 'why' (passion) you'll deal with any 'how' (circumstance). This is undoubtedly true because the human propensity for exploration, change, challenging the status quo, adaption, and innovation are all built on this strong survival drive. It seems logical that harnessing it to pursue career goals would make sense. We've already talked about dreams, and dreams are often passionate longings, aren't they?

The philosophical underpinnings:

To uncover the origins of this idea you won't spend a lot of time looking at business literature or the writings of great thinkers. Since this taps into such a powerful emotional spring in the human soul, you'll go where most flowery phrases and lofty aspirations arise- the human ability to tell a story. This ideal isn't from great organizational analysts like Demming or Drucker but comes out of poetry, film, novels, and children's literature. There is no definite source because it's part of the human psyche. One place to begin to unpack it is Joseph Campbell's The Hero's Journey which is one of many models to understand how a character progresses through a story. Generally speaking, there is a call to adventure, an answering of the call, a journey, and a return in the path of the narrative from beginning to end. The idea that each person's life is a unique journey with a personal calling from some force beyond rational comprehension is ultimately about the courage to take risks and a willingness to take responsibility for your actions. This 'embracing of destiny' is very epic in its tone and it does motivate some career management coaching methods. To lead a 'life of meaning' in those stories you have to find and go after that unique calling you have.

Why it doesn't always work:

Those who preach the effectiveness of 'follow your passions' often point to examples of successful people, sometimes themselves, as models of how this principle works. Follow the path of those who've gone on before and just stick to their program. If you're not fully aware, this can slip into a logical error referred to as "Survival Bias". At first glance, you might determine that Bill Gates, arguably one of the most successful men on the planet, dropped out of college and started a company so therefore this could be a path to success. However, it fails to account for multiple factors in his life that also contributed to his success. Circumstances of all kinds can prevent a person from pursuing what they might prefer to do. This story is far more common as life is rife with compromises.

Some people don't follow their passion because they just don't have one. There might be circumstances that severely limit their options, they're just too practical, or maybe just don't know how to express it. Since their story is less romantic than those of the passionate, you will rarely see it presented as a noble path worthy of dignity. Yet their path is noble and dignified all the same. Society just doesn't always see it that way because you can't use it to sell advertising.

In the end, the general reason the 'follow your passion' philosophy does not work as well as it could is that without a full understanding of how to follow this passion you won't get very far. It's understood that a passion that 'calls' to you isn't something that is written in the stars for you to find and that you are responsible for creating it. The call you hear is inside your brain. It's not outside you, it's inside. It's your vision and your plan. You are responsible for making it real. To accomplish that you require a lot of effort. If you're not willing to take responsibility to make it happen then it truly is no different than a dream you have while you're sleeping. You can follow a passion, but you have to be willing to pay the price. That's is often overlooked in the heroic stories; the hero pays a price and can never go back to their ordinary life after they're transformed by their journey. Those who preach 'follow your passion like I did' never really talk about how they had to leave some things behind in the process. What they do get right is that if you're fortunate enough to have a true passion, then we should recognize that you should be grateful for the opportunity this call presents.

Suggested Replacement:

"Follow Your Talents"

Passions are fraught with peril and they extract a heavy toll on the person who believes in them. What then can we do? Should we give it all up in favor of just doing what comes along?

No.

There is a more effective way to follow your passion. Passions can frequently place blinders on us so that we focus on meeting the milestones that help us stay on track to obtain our goals. Much has been written about this single-minded focus and building the associated habits of success that it overlooks what I think is an important question: What if you stop wanting what you once felt passionate about along the way?

When you aim for a target and hit it only to find that it's not what you thought it would be like, that the journey was better than the destination, that the dream was too small, or that there's more life left to live beyond the point when you achieved your passionate goal you have a choice to make. That choice is often to just give in or find a new passion. The first is the easy way out and the second is more challenging but worth it. The older you get though the more likely you are to accept that first choice. That is often a mistake though.

What if instead of following our passion, we decided to find be passionate about what we're doing? You are alive, you're unique, you can make choices regardless of any external factor. Our personal gifts, talents, and experiences shape us in distinct ways. We have unique skills and traits that are important enough to express to the larger world. These talents create strengths of character and ability that make life a joy to live when we recognize them, embrace them, and activate them. When following where our strengths are most helpful and most utilized we can discover that 'calling' that fires up our passion.

Listen to what your life has told you so far and see how it has made the world you live in today. From there, imagine this future world and future self you're working to build. You will ideally find that instead of an abstract vision of a perfect outside world you have a plan for making a world that builds on yesterday, lightens up the present, and encourages you to look forward to tomorrow.

Reconception: A New Model of Work

Now let's recap the 10 new ideas about work and how to use them as you manage your career.

1. Make your work matter
2. Enjoy your work.
3. Be eager to do hard things.
4. Showcase your ability to get results.
5. Show that you can learn.
6. A good job is an investment.
7. Make your own luck
8. Happiness comes from meaningful work.
9. Always be ready to change work.
10. Follow your talents.

In the previous chapters, we've spoken in generalized terms. We needed to help you understand that you possess an ability to take responsibility for where your career path is taking you. That action of responsibility and the understanding that you are fully capable of managing your career is foundational. You can change how you view your work and see it as an opportunity not only to impact the larger world but to provide a sense of personal satisfaction as well.

As stated earlier, these are not rules set in stone for all time. They are ideas that you can choose to adopt and use to frame how you view both your work and how you fit into the workplace. If work were a theatrical performance, these would be the set pieces and props that actors interact with and use to move the story along.

If the "stage is set" you could assume the next task now is to go out onto the stage and tell your story to your audience. We have some work to do first. Let's expand the acting metaphor a little more and discover that now that you have a story and framework of how things can be, the next step is to understand your character. This is not to say you have to pretend to be anything or play a role that is untrue. Character has a double meaning – it is both how people perceive you and your internal motivations. A person of disreputable character is regarded as one who says one thing but does another. A person of high character is one who is found to have integrity; what they do and choose is driven by their belief. A person's character is far more than belief or values, it is what is revealed in actions. No one can escape the discerning eyes of others because humans are social creatures hardwired to determine the level of an outsider's honesty and sense of fairness.

You have a moral and ethical character already. This could be something you have inherited as part of your culture, it could be one you've adopted as you've matured, or it could be one your own design you have crafted after much work. Character isn't optional because it's part of being human. We are going to sidestep most of the interpersonal and cultural issues though and focus on your vocational character- the 'you' that shows up to work each day and does the job required. We are focused here on the things about yourself that you're going to use to build a vision of your future work and what guides you as you create strategic goals and action plans.

Why all this internal work? Why can't we just skip right to the details of what needs doing? We certainly could, however, to truly find work that leads to meaning and fulfillment you must first understand what problems you're trying to solve by working. If your problem is merely a paycheck then by all means skip forward to the how-to sections. If you are frustrated by the rat race you find yourself then understand that you won't thrive as a confident person who takes pride in their work if you're just aiming to be a better-than-average rat. To escape the treadmill of meaningless work, you have to stop being a rat and be the type of human being you want to be instead.

The next section is about understanding yourself and the character you want to portray to the world. It is how you will connect with others and prove your relevance to their needs, which is the engine that drives the wheels of work. Once you see how you are motivated in a positive, prosocial way you can take the actions that allow you to meet the opportunities that come your way. The alternative is another boring job you use to pay the bills and pass time until you expire.

Section 3: Finding Your Career Character

"We have all a better guide in ourselves,

if we would attend to it,

than any other person can be."

— Jane Austen

Your Character M.A.P

In studying what has been written about success methods and successful people you will quickly find yourself chasing down a lot of blind alleys. Much is written about techniques and tactics for personal development and you don't have to look far online to find lists of deceptively simple things you can do to tip the odds of a successful outcome in favor of yourself.

The process of finding what you want to do next in your career and how to get there is centered on defining who you are and what you want. This exercise of understanding yourself better is a journey of self-discovery, built on the maxim that 'know thyself' as the beginning of knowledge. You might have tried this at one point yourself, resolving to get to the core of who you are and what drives you. You probably found out that it's really hard. This is why people like to skip this step but they skip it at their peril. We spend time doing it because the investment helps us make better decisions further along in the process. Our goal in the next section is to make it a little easier to accomplish by giving some guidelines and advice to direct you on the right path.

Why is it so difficult to know what we want and who we are? Perhaps the reason for this difficultly is that there is no solid 'me' that doesn't change. Change is what human beings do and it is what human beings in a sense are because it defines who we are. Imagine for a moment the life of someone who doesn't change. What would it look like? To know exactly everything about themselves and to be able to predict everything that happened because it never changes might actually be describing a curse, not a blessing. The Greek myth of Sysiphus describes a figure punished to eternally push a ball up a hill all day only to have it roll back down each night. What went through his mind each day? "Another day, another dollar"? "Same old, same old"? "Same stuff, different day"? (Sysiphus might have invented the novelty phrase office coffee mug.) If your life is like Sysiphus, then you already know that it's no fun.

We are not cursed to roll a ball uphill though. Rather than seeing life as predetermined and success as something outside ourselves, what would it be like if we embraced the change that is inside us and all around us? Learning about the world doesn't just mean knowing details about it but rather is about experiencing the world as it is. Learning is about being changed, in thought and action, by the knowledge you acquire. Knowing yourself should change not just how you see yourself but should actually change who you are. Keep that in mind and let's move on from the philosophy into how this actually impacts your career choices.

In the career field, the nature of the self and the unpredictability of personality is problematic to a degree. If you're marketing your career assets to a potential employer, they will review your professional reputation and the narrative you present as they would a branded product. While you are a unique set of experiences on this planet you need to have a thematic story of who you are to be able to explain that to people. While you can know yourself fairly well, you have to be able to share this story of who you are and, more importantly, who you want to be, in order to be persuasive enough to connect with people.

Who you choose to become in your career not only guides your choices, actions, and outcomes but also reveals to others what you're trying to do and why you're doing it. It motivates you, drives you to excel, guides your choices, and when you stray from where you're longing to be you'll feel a sense of discomfort that will draw you back. To achieve at the highest level, you must go beyond thinking of how you work as just something you do, but rather a reflection of who you want to be at your best. Your career then is ideally defined by your ***character.***

Character maps are used in theatre to help diagram how an actor makes choices in portraying a character. It helps the actor understand what the playwright was intending as they wrote and use their own understanding of motivation and human response to inform how they choose to portray the character to the audience. In career coaching, a career map can help you see the different strategic choices you can make. We combine these two seemingly separate tools into one wholistic guide we call the **Career Character MAP.**

In a career-sense individual character breaks down into three parts – **Mission, Attitude, and Purpose.** These three elements combine to guide your work with something that will keep you moving forward and provide you with a sense of pride in both good and bad times.

How do we uncover our missions, attitudes, and purposes? We start by defining these three aspects of our character by doing what coaches do best: ask questions and measure those answers against performance. There are five questions that can help you better understand yourself and see how you're doing. Once you have walked through and answered these questions you should be empowered to craft a strategic plan for your career which you can implement through practical action steps. It will ideally also feel 'right'.

We don't want to ask just any questions though. We need to get down to the basic principles of what drives you as a person. We want to focus not on our faults but on our strengths and talents, what is best about us and what is positive. Organizations do this and craft strategic plans that guide their activities and missions. The most effective operations are driven by their Mission, leverage their Attitude, and fulfill their Purpose for their customers and their own sustainability. Peter Drucker developed 5 questions to help businesses find their mission and we've come up with a similar list of 5 questions to help you create that strategic edge in your career.

Your Mission is the 'what' of "what are you trying to build?" Nothing gets done without other people, so these questions are about how you connect with other people. You don't have to be a do-gooder or martyr to have a mission in life. It is the spice that helps you enjoy things because it helps bring joy to others. More importantly, Mission creates a sense of personal culture that serves as a set of boundaries and a guide to what actions are helpful and what ones will set you back. Culture is what facilitates organizational strategy and is no less true on the personal level. Your Mission is your guide to connecting with others.

Your Mission is built on just two questions:

Question 1: What do you want? (to achieve for yourself and others)?

Question 2: What can you do for others? (Nothing gets done without people)

Your Attitude is how you feel, emotionally and rationally, about yourself and your skills that you're using to accomplish your Mission. Do you take pride in what you're doing in the present? What have you done in the past that needs to be shared with others? What do you treasure about yourself (your talents), what is unique to your personality/history (your strengths), and what is most important to you (your values)? You get to choose the Attitude you want to be known for through your work. This is what you want to offer others, including your current or future employers, so you can be an asset to them as well. You should feel good about what you've accomplished. As Zig Ziglar once said, "Your attitude, not your aptitude, will determine your altitude". Your attitude should ultimately convey confidence and self-assurance to those you're looking to help.

Your Attitude is found by asking the questions:

Question 3: What can you do? (Your abilities)

Question 4: What have you done? (Your history)

The idea of Purpose can trip people up, but it shouldn't. That can happen when it is used as a stand-in for what we're calling 'meaning' here. A purpose is not the grand attribute that is written once and for all on a person's destiny. While a romantic and noble view, it isn't necessarily helpful to individuals trying to figure out what they want to accomplish. How we use it in this sense is that your Purpose is defined by, and is a synonym for, your goals. Purpose here is not just a reason for existence, it's a reason to exist; you have something you need to do. Your Purpose is chosen and never final, just as goals are. The key attribute of Purpose is that it aligns with your Mission and your Attitude. You show your purpose by what you're doing today.

Your Purpose is defined by one question based on the previous four:

Question 5. What are you doing to make this happen? (present action)

What do you do with these three once you've sorted them out? Add them together and you'll find something that most people spend their entire lives looking for: *Meaning*

Meaning = Mission + Attitude + Purpose

Meaning is what drives us to take the actions that we take, from getting out of bed to going the extra mile. Our actions are sacrifices large and small of effort and attention and Meaning is what makes them rewarding. If you craft your Meaning deliberately then you will find inspiration in those actions that can drive you even farther than you once thought possible. Human life needs meaning like it needs water. That meaning can be as simple as 'I provide for my family' to as grand as 'I want to be the first person to set foot on Mars'. It takes what we're trying to do and who we are in combination with actionable goals to move us towards achievement. The result of all the effort should be a life of meaning during the pursuit of our mission. Ideally, our meaning goes beyond the default social meaning of "I want to fully fund my retirement" to whatever it is provides them with the satisfaction, contentment, and happiness found in doing good work.

The best part of the process is that we have some say in how we express them in our lives. If for example you examine yourself and find they don't add up in a way that makes sense or in a way that's just not you, you can change the meaning by changing the component parts that make up that meaning. Change the things that you're doing or the answers you're getting until it adds up the way you need it to. It's your life after all.

In the next chapters, we're going to walk through each question in order. After each, we will give you a series of exercises to work through to help you determine what your answer might be. It may sound tough, and it might be if you're not used to being honest with yourself, but it's worth the investment of time. Don't be afraid to walk through these questions with a trusted advisor or coach because an outsider's perspective can assist you in forming a full picture of who you are and what you're trying to do.

Career Character M.A.P.

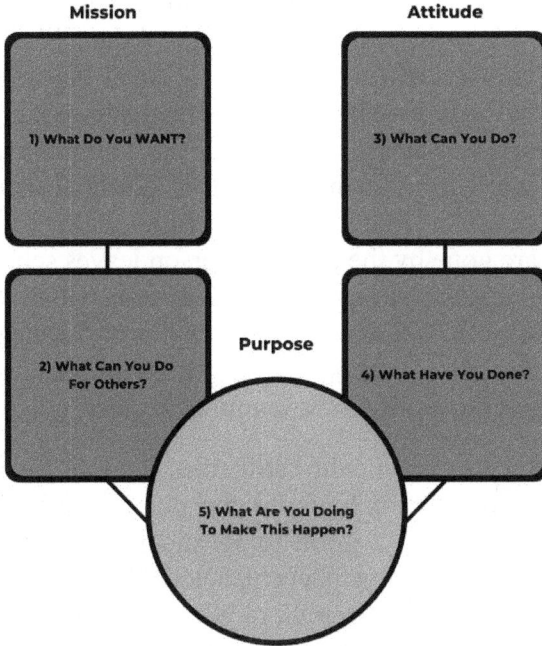

Mission

Attitude

1) What Do You WANT?

3) What Can You Do?

Purpose

2) What Can You Do For Others?

4) What Have You Done?

5) What Are You Doing To Make This Happen?

M.A.P Question #1 "What Do You Want?"

This question seems to be tougher than it actually is. The most common answers we come up with at first are: "I don't know" or "something that's not this". Often the reason this question is so difficult to answer is that we put far too much importance on its answer. We might also be a little afraid of the answer.

When we were children, the answer came readily. We might, for example, answer "I want to be an Olympic Athlete!" at a very early age and, given our lack of awareness of what that might require, believe it's totally do-able because our imaginations can conceive it. As we got older, we started to encounter the world in a more mature fashion and we learn that imagination is essential, but so is hard work and sacrifice. Many times, dreams born of the young imagination are gone by the time the person leaves school, replaced by a drive to make a large quantity of cash. Goals born of the imagination are replaced with goals born out of practicality. This is mostly by design as schooling is often architected to create compliance and the ability to be useful to society.

That compliance to practicality still rules the day for many of us, sometimes for our entire lives, to the point it defines our lives. Practicality is certainly a good thing and is born of the cardinal virtue the ancient philosophers labeled 'Prudentia' (origin of Prudence in English) and serves to elevate the ideal that wisdom should be practical (Prudentia is sometimes translated as 'practical wisdom'). You can say that practical wisdom is knowing that pumpkins and tomatoes don't belong in a fruit basket even though they are also fruits.

Practicality is an abused virtue when it's used to lie. We're lying to ourselves when we say that we're being practical when in reality we are being either complacent or fearful. We all, either at times or as a way of life, go through our days and don't dream too much because we mistakenly believe grownups only think in these practical terms, never in 'dreams'. When imagination does try to capture our attention, we excuse it away and say 'life gets in the way' of doing much about it. Because of this, we define our careers by what we can do and have done, but never take much time to think about what we want. Wanting something is important and ought not to be overlooked. Regardless of whether what you want is a small or a large order, it's important because it's what will both guide our goals and serve as our legacy. Practicality and imagination both need us to move out of our comfort zone. Imagination because it is the faculty that we need for empathy, adaptability, and innovation. Practicality needs us to get uncomfortable because not taking risks, even the risk of wanting something, is to stop growing and become a worker drone going through the motions of life. This is both overly materialistic, philosophically fatalistic, and functionally nihilistic – all attributes of antisocial and self-destructive behavior.

'Wanting' something is how we give our lives the drive that we need to act on the goals required to make things happen. Businesses want to make a profit, it's why they exist. Nonprofit organizations want to solve a problem in society. Every person who gets up and goes to work do so because they want something, often that's as simple as getting paid. Regardless of what it is, you have to first want to do something before you do it. This is the very definition of motivation and being motivated is what drives us to take action. Even if you think you don't want to do something, if you're actually doing it you want something. That motivation can be internal, meaning it comes from a need inside yourself, or external, meaning it comes from an outside motivator. Internal motivators might be a sense of achievement while external motivators would be things such as money.

Internal motivation is easier to sustain over time. If you're drowning or trapped in a burning building, you'll be motivated by your internal survival instinct to escape the circumstances and live to see another day. Nobody has to threaten you with a stick or bribe you with a carrot to come out of the flames. Internal motivation is a strong force if we can tap into it. I believe one of the reasons we do is we don't tap tap into this power is that we fail to see our desires as part of a larger whole. Let's say you want a fried fish sandwich for lunch, you might have the cash and the ability to obtain that sandwich, so what is preventing you from having that greasy fried delight for lunch? Your doctor might be stopping you for one if they've told you to stop having fried foods. Your spouse and children might be another because they want you to eat healthier. You might also be the sort of person who eats what they shouldn't and then pays a biological price later that causes them to regret a choice. Those external motivators might stop you. Ultimately though if you personally want to eat healthily you'll choose not to give in to the urge to eat the fish. If you really didn't care, you might give into temptation.

This is why "What do you want" is just the beginning. To make a truly wise choice that promotes the welfare of yourself, those you care about, and those around you in the community you have to have some practicality. That's why in the end this question is really "What do you want to achieve" when talking about careers. Achievement is focused forward into the future and this will come into play again once we reach later. For now, it is enough to remember that wanting something involves an investment of effort and material that has to pay off in the future in a way that outweighs any regrets your projected future self might have about your choice.

At certain times (middle age, post-college, nearing retirement, etc.) we all realize that our lives are short and that we can only spend so much of it living for the dreams and desires of someone else. Sadly, not everyone gets this luxury so for those who do it's vitally important to listen to their consciences and make the changes necessary to avoid wasting the precious opportunities we encounter. This is oftentimes when imagination comes back in a very strong way, but practicality demands we still pay the power bill each month. While imagination gives us a view into what could be, practicality grounds to us the reality that we also have a responsibility to take care of ourselves and those who count on us. Balancing these two responsibilities, to not waste our lives and to be responsible for ourselves, is a good starting point of career goal setting. You have to balance them to guide the hard choices you need to make in order to move forward. By remaining centered on these you are able to activate the internal motivation needed to make progress.

How does this work? Being emotionally invested in your goals will help you formulate and activate a plan that is easier to stick to. Think of it as you would a diet. (Yeah, diets again) If you have a diet that includes only healthy options, but you don't like them, you'll have a hard time staying on track. If you have a diet of only the things you want, but they have zero health value, you'll find it easy to stick to but also get very sick. The former is a working life that is 100% practical, the latter is one that is 100% imagination. Balancing good choices will drastically improve your odds of success because you care. By caring and being emotionally committed, you might think you are just risking disappointment, but the truth is without caring you have no reason to complete what you set out to and chances of success are slim. If you do succeed, what's the point if you don't feel good about it? Knowing what you want is the first step in defining your goals. If you can find inspiration that feeds your soul, attaining them will be more enjoyable. We all want to do the things in life we find enjoyable and that motivates us. But how does this focus us outward instead of inward? This is supposed to be about our Mission in our work, right?

When you want something, you will be required to engage with other people. Anything that gets done requires, at one point or another, the assistance of other human beings. That's by design if you look at both the natural order and society in general. While your wants, hopes, dreams, responsibilities, and survival needs all start with you they definitely end with connecting to others. In the career strategy world, there are many steps to take once you've defined what you want. A coach or strategic planner might help you use the common models such as GROW, SWOT, PEST or SMART to set goals, metrics, and accountability plans. But to put them into action you're going to need to connect with other people.

Walt Disney said it best: "You can design and create and build the most wonderful place in the world. But it takes people to make the dream a reality." While at a conference in Orlando I stayed at a hotel that was across from Walt Disney World and my room overlooked the entire Disney property. The massive scale of this enterprise was breathtaking because unlike a city that grew organically this was completely planned. Castles, mountains, and resorts all were planted in what had been a long-ignored swamp all because one man had a vision and convinced others that it was worth the effort. It would still be empty land if not for other people though. His imagination saw an amazing testament to human endeavor and his practical side saw that it would take building an organization to support it. He also saw that both of these things required people. This vision outlasted him because what he wanted inspired others to want something too.

In the world of work, regardless if a person works as an employee or an entrepreneur, you can rarely see goals achieved or pave the way for them without getting others to buy into your vision. That vision can be as simple as 'I can do the job' or as grand as 'I will outperform everyone else and rise to the very top'. By sharing your vision for the future you'll find that goals can become reality because people will want to connect with you and help you. This is an emotional act that taps into a fundamental drive we all have to listen to stories. Your story is performed on a public stage on a daily basis. Your audience wants to feel what you feel and can easily tell if your heart really isn't in your dream.

If you know what you want, it's up to you to figure out what the steps are to get you there. You will find help along the way if you ask for it. You need other people, so wanting something and being able to share that want is how you connect and you will also find yourself wanting to help other people fulfill their goals too. That's how it becomes part of your Mission, you start helping others as you help yourself. Because, in the end, we're all in this together.

Question #1 Activity

How would you honestly answer these questions?

*   Write down your answers, then set them aside. Come back to them a short time later and re-answer them.
*   Repeat the previous step until you create at least 3 sets of answers.
*   Compare them and you should find the 3rd set resonates as the most truthful to you.

1) What could change in your life and make it better?

2) What did you want when you were younger that you stopped pursuing?

3) What would you change about yourself that would make you a better person?

M.A.P. Question #2 "What Can You Do for Others?"

Whatever you decide to do is going to take assistance from someone else. As Zig Ziglar once said, "You can have everything in life you want if you just help other people get what they want." Taking action on goals requires that you connect with the right people that you can help and can help you in return. Let's start by looking at this from a purely personal level.

The world of work is much like a marketplace in the sense that it is transactional in nature. In order to get something, you have to give something. Applied to a career, this means that in order to gain a position at an organization you have to demonstrate the value of your experience, your skills, and why getting what you want (in this case, the job) is beneficial to both. Ideally, both the career seeker and employer will understand this transaction as an investment- the time spent by both parties is not just buying skills but increasing the capacity for the benefit of all parties.

In the broad scheme of things, helping other people is not just all about the paycheck. To connect to people is more than communicating value and exchanging it for what you need. A connection is social in nature and groups of people form up around ideals and ethical principles. You see that in social movements, electoral politics, fandoms, and spirituality. People have an innate instinct to cluster in groups centered around mutual interests, opinions, and cultures. Our consumer-centric and organizational models used to be focused on individuals as rational actors whose sole decided factor was self-interest. In the Digital Age though the person is seen as a unique entity that has shared traits with the groups they belong to. You can see evidence of this in the way ubiquitous social media algorithms attempt to classify people into categories to hyper-customize advertising experiences. From the viewpoint of an individual's career, it is important to take those who you want to cluster with and those you want to serve into consideration.

This does not mean you should isolate yourself to only your preferred group, it should imply the opposite. The reason you don't want to only stay with your group is that you can create a feedback loop, sometimes called an epistemological bubble, that will harm your ability to connect in the long term. Likewise, on the individual level you don't only want to seek out those who you want to work with. Diversity and openness is a survival strategy when it comes to connections. Never dismiss anyone's value just as you do not wish to be dismissed. You can and should remain firm in your personal boundaries though and respect those of others. When you find that level of balance, you will find it not only easier to communicate and connect but you will also find it a healthier social practice.

But how do you make that connection? Are you essentially just selling yourself with an elevator pitch? Thankfully, you're not. People aren't widgets or products to be 'branded', they are organizational assets that work in partnership with the rest of the team and the organization's overall mission. To build that kind of connection starts not with a pitch, selling, or persuasive parlor tricks but by 1) listening to what problems a person/organization is having and 2) being genuinely engaged with the people and process.

Listening in the job search is about learning what challenges and issues need to be addressed by the person in the position. Too often people pitch themselves as the best solution without taking the time to hear what the problem actually is. The listening step can't be avoided because as sales expert Kerwin Rae points out "Solutions only derive their value from the problems they solve". Your value to an employer isn't just that you align with all the checkboxes in the job posting but that you are willing to help them solve the problems the organization faces. The benefit to the candidate is that you also learn if you are, in fact, the best answer to their problem. Never forget that both the candidate and employer must agree that they're a good match before anyone commits to the investment of employment. Listening is what prevents costly employment missteps.

Fortunately listening is an easy skill to learn, it just requires a conscious application of attention. Think of a time you were at a party and chatted with a person who talked only about themselves? Was it fun? Probably not and it was memorable in a bad way. Think of another time where the person seemed truly interested in what you had to say. Chances are this was a more enjoyable memory. Listening is just that simple and you will find as you do it that it also makes you feel better about your interactions. In a job search, you'll use it most often in networking and interviews, but it's a skill worth investing in for the long term as well. To master this skill, try to consciously pay attention when around others by listening to what people are saying then ask questions to help you understand their point of view better. This works well online too.

While listening is something that we are all familiar with, personal engagement is a little more confusing. Functionally, you can define it as the way we participate in a task. What does it mean in a personal sense though? How do you know if you're engaged with a job/employer/task? In a blunt and practical sense, you can boil it to this: "Do you care?" Engagement is a formal business-speak word for emotional involvement because most of us are culturally trained to avoid emotions in the workplace. While it's important to be professional in all things, it's impossible to simply turn off emotions like a light switch. Understanding how you feel about a situation will help you identify how to leverage your strengths and talents to the best of your ability. Feeling good about your work doesn't make it less challenging, but it does make it more enjoyable for yourself and those around you. It will be what creates that honest connection between people even when you don't necessarily feel that your heart is in the game.

Engagement matters to the job seeker because by showing you care you're broadcasting that you're both energized and open to new challenges and ideas. In the most ideal scenario, the 'you' that others experience during your interactions in the interview are ideally a preview of how you react in the workplace and carry a far greater weight in the decision process than factors on your resume. While this isn't always the case, however, a genuine and honest interaction by all parties is a good predictor of personal job 'fit'. A job that fits well by encouraging you to be your best self is a valuable commodity because emotional well-being makes the effort invested in a job more satisfying.

If you're listening and you're engaged, you will hopefully discover that your career trajectory is on the proper course. You might also find, however, that it's not. Be certain the employer or client you connect with is listening in return. It is never equal, sometimes you have to listen more than you are heard but don't let your voice be totally silenced. Life is too short to invest extra effort in a job or for a group you that doesn't drive your Mission forward. Be ready to pivot on to someone who listens to what you're saying.

Question #2 Activity

How would you honestly answer these questions?

- Write down your answers, then set them aside.
- Come back to them a short time later and re-answer them.
- Repeat the previous step until you create at least 3 sets of answers.
- Compare them and you should find the 3rd set resonates as the most truthful to you.

1) Who do you want to help?

2) When you were younger, who's help did you need?

3) What is a problem in the world you wish someone would try to fix? How could you help?

M.A.P. Question 3: "What Can You Do?"

We've looked at how your Mission interacts with other people, so now let's look at what you have that you can use to get you to your intended goals and to serve others. Let's dive into your greatest career asset and the one thing that can't be taken from you. That's your ability to make a choice and do something about your circumstances. The best place to start is where you are right now. This question and the next are about your Performance – the 'do' in "So, what do you do?" Getting a grounding in what you are capable of, talented in, and what you enjoy doing makes sure that "So, what do you do?" doesn't become "so what". As you consider what direction to chart your future actions, you might become overwhelmed with the myriad of possibilities you have. The good news is that this is normal. It's called the Paradox of Choice; the more choice you have the less choice you seem to have.

The bad news is that as an adult managing your own career you still have to pick a path. This isn't always true for everybody, sometimes career paths are prescribed by circumstance, previous choices, education/experience, or the simple fact that you know where you want to go. Choices here are easy because there isn't much of one. But some have a strong desire to blaze their own path and, knowingly or unknowingly, welcome the opportunity to choose. Sometimes a person skips back-and-forth between both feast and famine of choice. Regardless of which camp you fall into, the necessity for using both goals and a strategic action plan once that choice is made is not optional.

You don't have to be alone in the process. Seeking assistance outside your own point of view is helpful along the way. This might take the form of reading books, listening to TED talks, podcasts, school career centers, or getting advice from family and friends. Some will take the path of enlisting the services of a personal career coach to help guide them. Earl Nightingale once said that achieving goals boiled down to a simple process: "All you need is the plan, the road map, and the courage to press on to your destination". The role of the career coach is in helping to create the road map. It's the guide that the client uses to direct their actions and, in time, achieve the results they want. Then they also help you find the courage to get moving.

Just as no two people are alike, there are no two job paths that are the same. What a coach will do, and you should do if you're coaching yourself, is to focus on unlocking your personal preferences and abilities through a process of questioning. This will help you get a better understanding not just of where you're going but where you've been and what you have to offer. Why all the questions? Because it's often the best way to find the answer to personal problems. Robert Kiyosaki said it best: "A question opens the mind. A statement closes the mind". Asking questions opens up the possibilities of what a person can do. While not every coach follows the same process, I have found that before you set a goal it's best to start by understanding the person as they are now. In a simple sense, it's determining where you're at before figuring out where you're going. Trainers and educators will do this to ascertain at what level the learner is working and what knowledge they possess before deciding on the instructional challenges to give them. If you want to be CEO, but you're currently working in the mailroom, you'll naturally set different goals than someone who's already a vice president.

We can start with "What can you do?" to help us get to know what talents and skills the person already possesses. This is the foundation of both resume writing and career coaching because not only do we get a better grasp of the whole person, but the process also gives the client a better understanding of themselves. This honest look at themselves is not always a comfortable process at first. By going through it, the resulting inventory of internal resources is helpful in understanding both your present position in the job market and giving you insight into how you engage in the workplace.

One of the best tools you might use to start this process is Gallup's CliftonStrengths assessment. Unlike traditional personality tests, the CliftonStrengths (formerly StrengthsFinder) is truly centered on the individual in their career or work setting and is based on solid data. We use it to help discover how clients do their best work and what approaches they can use to develop their talents into strengths. Focusing on what's right, instead of what's wrong, allows a person to lean into their strengths and fix them as the directional guide for their goals. We call this 'Fixing what's right with you'. Knowing how you work helps to find interests, patterns of behavior, and possible pitfalls that emerge out of these traits to display a bigger picture of how you 'operate'.

Beyond internal resources, also do an inventory of the professional skills a person has developed. While education and technical skills are important, professional habits always win out over them both. If you've ever hired the wrong person for the right reasons, meaning they worked out great on paper but were a hot mess to work with, then you understand this principle all too well. This piece of the puzzle helps to determine how a person engages with their work. This engagement element is a critical factor in future success. In the business sense 'engagement' has many definitions, but as we've said before it ultimately boils down to how much you actually care about what you're doing. From the career coaching standpoint, this engagement is critical in the job change process because it drives the outcomes of the effort. Some would call it a 'brand', but branding is what you do for a product or livestock. In a career-sense, it can be thought of as a personal culture that serves as a hallmark to your work and is the fuel for all strategic advancement towards a goal, so it's important to understand how you show up. As Peter Drucker correctly surmised: "Culture eats strategy for breakfast." Having an understanding of what you care about gives you insight into your cultural style so you can know what to look for, and what to avoid when weighing your career options. No amount of planning or strategy can survive if it does not accurately reflect the culture it exists in.

"What can you do?" is a broad enough question that it could almost be the only one to use when planning a career strategy. Like a building's blueprints however you can see the outline of what could be, but not the entire structure. Goals serve as great endpoints to direct the trip, but unless you know where you're starting from, you'll never know what route to take.

Question #3 Activity

ProTip: Consider taking the Gallup CliftonStrengths Assessment and engaging with a Certified Strengths Coach to help you understand, embrace, and direct your unique talents.

How would you honestly answer these questions?

- Write down your answers, then set them aside.
- Come back to them a short time later and re-answer them.
- Repeat the previous step until you create at least 3 sets of answers.
- Compare them and you should find the 3rd set resonates as the most truthful to you.

1) What can you do better than most people?

2) What do you enjoy doing?

3) How you do view the world differently from others?

4) What does your resume say about your abilities?

M.A.P. Question #4 "What Have You Done?"

You could presume that once you've discovered where you are on the map of your career by looking at what you can do, it's time to determine your destination. There's an extra step that needs to be taken before going forward. We looked at your talents, skills, and strengths- now let's look into what has gotten you where you are today. Every person also has a backstory and knowing where you've been can help to light the path to where you're headed. Your work history is always understood as where you've been and what you've done. You might think of your career like a spacecraft hurtling through the cosmos and you are Mission Control in charge of all the flight details. If your ship took off from Earth, heading to Mars, and you wanted to know how much flight time you have until you get there you would apply some basic math to determine where it is in relation to Earth and Mars. In a similar way, you can look at where your career started, how you've progressed, how much 'fuel' you have left, and then determine if you're going to make your goals any time soon.

Practically speaking, this starts with taking a look at the record of work and accomplishments a person has achieved up to the present. The best place to do that is your resume (sometimes spelled resumé) or CV. Most people dread their resumes. It's understandable because much like in Question 1 there's a lot of self-reflection that occurs. Fortunately, and paradoxically, while a resume is about you it's not actually about you. Your resume establishes your validity as a candidate to interested parties by showcasing your accomplishments. Once that validity is established, then there's potential for connection. From that connection comes trust. From that trust, a partnership can be built.

So how do you showcase yourself? It's not something we're trained to do in society because it often seems to go against pro-social values such as humility and selflessness. While it can go down the path of bragging when a novice writes a resume, a good writer can make a document both humble and oriented towards the reader. How do you do that? Simply state what you've done and the impact it's had in an honest manner. Honesty isn't bragging when it is a statement of fact. Taking pride in your accomplishments isn't the bad version of pride, it's the healthy kind. Songwriter Mac McAnally explains it this way: "Take pride in what you do for a living even if you have a job that sucks because that's the quickest way to a job that sucks less." Honest confidence and healthy pride in demonstrated achievements are what the reader needs to see.

Writing a resume is difficult for some of us because we can't always know how others perceive us without external feedback. Think of how often in today's marketing-centric culture we roll our eyes at someone without the self-awareness to realize what a Grade A idiot they're making of themselves? Can't think of an example? Spend 5 minutes on Twitter or Facebook and you'll find at least one. In the example, you find the person in question doesn't necessarily perceive what they're communicating as being an issue, but you did. Which is right then? Marketing of anything (soap, cars, TV shows, or a person's job history) is built on a rule: "perception is reality". You perceived them as out-of-touch. As the audience, your opinion and assessment will always rule out over their intention. Resumes are like that. You might think "I'm a shoo-in for this job!". The hiring manager, your audience, might think differently.

Have you ever accidentally acted in a way that in retrospect is perceived as boorish or insulting? There's a good chance that the realization you'd been insulting was because a well-meaning person was looking out for you and told you of your unintended transgression. The value of an honest broker to help guide you and create an understanding of yourself cannot be understated because as you create the message that is your career story, you want your intentions to be understood by others. Nobody can understand what's going on in your brain or your life without using words. Choosing the right words often means looking for help to ensure they are understood. A well-crafted message is easier to share than a half-hearted attempt.

When analyzing your resume, there are a lot of basic details to cover that are too numerous to mention here. What is important when answering this question is looking at what kind of career you have had up until this point and time, listing out your accomplishments, then seeing what story you've been telling through your outcomes.

Your message is built of what you've been doing, and your actions are the author of the story you're trying to tell.

Start with auditing your career up until the present day. This can be the largest part of the writing process. Most will start by compiling a chronological list of their positions and what the responsibilities and job descriptions were. This is a good place to begin for certain, but it's important to not stop here. Why? Because put yourself in the position of a hiring manager, interviewer, or HR data-scanning algorithm. Too much data that's not relevant to what you need to know is tossed out. In that process of tossing out the bad, a lot of good may go with it. Let's say you're buying a toaster online that you're going to use for bagels. When you start searching through the products offered do you want to read the entire manual for each item, or would you prefer to just scan the page and find the ones that have a 'bagel' setting? Now if you're hiring for a position that has the X, Y, and Z experience then you'll waste a lot of time if you have to read through A, B, C, D,... to get through to X, Y, Z. Get to the point and stick to it by highlighting the most important data about yourself that speaks to objective accomplishment.

Why can't we just rely on the basic facts though? We rely on data and metrics in organizations to drive decisions frequently. There is a multitude of reasons, first and foremost is that data never shows the whole picture. Communication requires connection but also requires context. We can transmit information easily (connection), but to ensure that it's understood requires the ability to tell a story (context). This is why resumes aren't easy to write, they require an understanding of the person being written about to properly show the person is more than just a widget, but an asset worthy of investment. The phrase "the map is not the territory" can be expanded to say, "The resume is not the person".

This isn't to say it's hopeless to write one. Quite the opposite is true: it should be written well and updated often. The document serves as a record of personal achievement, a barometer of current intention, and trajectory of future growth. A good resume not only shows a person's technical skill but also crafts a narrative of a person. From there, a reader can decide whether or not to connect with them. A resume won't get you a job. However, it will show who you are and what you've accomplished. To get where you want to go, you have to know where you are and what you've accomplished so far. The resume is the narrative tool that will showcase your relevance.

Your resume isn't just a piece of paper you only bring out in the job interview. Your resume is a stand-in for *you*. It is a written record of your history and reputation. Your actions are the living resume you are writing each day by the way you do your work. To do work get offered work that allows you not just to fulfill your mission but help you perform at your peak, you have to show how you perform to those you are serving. That is what is going to open the doors you need to pass through on your way to your next goal.

Question #4 Activity

How would you honestly answer these questions?

- Write down your answers, then set them aside.
- Come back to them a short time later and re-answer them.
- Repeat the previous step until you create at least 3 sets of answers.
- Compare them and you should find the 3rd set resonates as the most truthful to you.

1) Write out your professional biography – how does it look to you?

2) At what point in your life did you feel the most competent?

3) What kind of impact have you made in the past?

M.A.P. Question #5 "What Are You Doing to Make This Happen?"

This question serves as a bridge between what you're trying to do (Mission) and what tools you have to accomplish it (Attitude). You can view this as the part where two circles overlap in a Venn diagram – you need the other two parts for it to exist. The goals that you will use to guide your strategy and keep you on-track (Purpose) begin here.

Let's walk through how this question might play out in a hypothetical scenario. Say that you want to help those in need in your hometown because you don't want anyone to experience hunger. You have a passion for horseback riding, strong organizing skills, a talent for business analysis, experience leading training, and a reputation for running tech companies. You have come to a crossroads where you have decided to reinvent what you're doing in a way to solve this problem (community hunger).

You narrow down your next steps to the following three options:

1. Launch a tech company that helps people find the least expensive fresh food in areas designated as food deserts.
2. Become a partner in a horse ranch and teach people to ride.
3. Work as a fund developer at a non-profit food pantry for your local community.

Which might you choose?

- Option one does speak to a lot of what you can do and have done. It directly addresses the hunger issue but involves a lot of work and risk.
- Option two would be fun but doesn't really solve the problem of hunger and uses only a portion of your talents.
- Option three is direct to your intended mission but doesn't align as well with your background or experience.

Which is the right answer? As we've seen before, there is no one answer that is absolutely correct. You could choose any of them. How do you decide then?

One way is to visualize each future scenario and work backward to determine what steps will take you there. You might also weigh the pros and cons of each scenario to determine what is most important. You could consult a coach or trusted advisor to give you feedback. The choice is yours to make. One of the most sought-after commodities in the world is not gold, power, or wealth but clarity. Entire departments of data scientists pour over mountains of data hoping to remove risk out of organizational decision making. As an individual, you don't have the resources or time to waste on being as close to certain as you can get. For the individual, it comes down to making a choice based on the best available data you have and pulling the proverbial trigger.

Clarity is found in hindsight, not always in foresight. The outcome of this question is that you have a decision to make and when you arrive later on down the road you look back to see how far you've come. The subtext of this question could be listed as "Is what you're doing producing the results you need?" Check your goals against both who you're helping and what energizes you frequential to make sure they are aligned. If they are not, make the changes you need to ensure your actions and investments are producing the outcomes necessary to keep you on track. This question is designed to keep you honest about what you're working towards in a real and tangible sense so that what you spend your effort on produces the outcomes you need them to.

Question #5 Activity

Start by collecting your final answers from the 4 previous activities.

1) How do you feel about the direction you are heading at present?

2) Do you feel that the activities and motivations you currently have are in alignment?

3) Is the direction you're heading in helping to produce a result you care about?

Strategy = Adding it all up

Now let's look at a question that doesn't always have an answer. That question is "does what you're doing have any meaning?"

Meaning is like success; it varies from person to person. It is much like the elephant in the parable of The Elephant and the Blind Men. Each man had a different take on the elephant's traits. One thought it was a snake because they felt the trunk, another said it was like a plant because of its ears, and so forth. You might think you have the most important and meaningful job in the world, but others could view what you do as a joke or worse. Everyone has their own take on meaning.

Meaning is also much like happiness in that it cannot be directly sought. It is the outcome or byproduct of your actions and intentions. From the viewpoint of your work when your Mission, Attitude, and Purpose are all working in harmony you will most likely find it easy to say you have meaning in your work. When we work from our strengths we more easily get into a state of flow. In this way, your sense of meaning is created and brought to our work, not found inside of it.

Meaning is your vision for what you want your life to become and the type of world you want to build for yourself and others.

That is work worth doing, isn't it?

Why should we even care about meaning? Life is short and what we do to earn a living doesn't always matter, does it? Actually, it does. People are inexorably connected in infinitely complex ways and the way you engage, the way you demonstrate your character, the way you work, are like ripples in a pond that intersect with a multitude of other ripples. Your actions and intentions matter right now, at this moment. Don't worry about tomorrow, or even if your work will matter when you're gone. The meaning of your work is having an impact right now on yourself and on everyone you are connected to. We work to survive. We also work to live a life that has meaning. Sometimes that meaning is as simple as a job well done. If you're lucky, it is much bigger.

You've spent time in the preceding exercises examining yourself, imagining what options you have, and now you have to get going. Take action on what you've learned and as time goes on take stock of both how you're progressing and how what you're doing aligns with your goals. Alter your course and activities as needed. Importantly, never be afraid to reinvent what you're doing if you want. You can make changes in yourself and your character because there's no reason not to.

Section 4: Career Tactics – Writing Your Resume

"Strive not to be a success, but rather to be of value."

— *Albert Einstein*

Embracing the 'Next Normal'

The phrase 'new normal' is thrown around a lot whenever there is massive social upheaval. It implies that once we get through the disruption that we will get back to things being 'normal' but slightly different because we've changed. While it's accurate, the phrase we prefer to use when talking about career management is the 'Next Normal'. We call it that because 'normal' is a moving target and always changing. Disruption and reinvention should not only be expected but planned for. We should always be prepared to adapt and embrace change that keeps the cycle of renewal going.

In the previous chapters, you have spent time understanding why you need to manage your career, looking at a new way to approach your career, and finally embracing what your strategy might look like. In this next section we will talk about the tools you need to make your career, and professional self, more resilient and produce the results you want. These are the 'nuts and bolts' and the tools of the career management trade you can use to consistently and predictably reinvent your relevance in the workplace.

We will start with writing your resumé (which we will spell as "resume" from this point forward), then look at your crafting search strategy, and finally looking at the best ways to prepare for an interview.

Always remember:

The best time to plan your career was yesterday,

the second-best time is today,

the worst time is tomorrow.

What is a resume anyway?

At the most basic of levels, a resume is a chronological listing of previous employment and other relevant data written to provide an overview of a person's previous accomplishments and skills.

While you can certainly start there, you definitely don't want to stop there! Why? Because there is a word for resumes like that:

Boring.

A Modern resume is a different beast. Modern resumes need to focus on accomplishments over simple data. Why? Because raw data doesn't tell a story or communicate value. A modern resume communicates what you can bring to a potential employer, which is why a modern resume is not a simple recounting of history that consists of each job you've held the descriptions of duties.

Did you notice in neither of the preceding descriptions did we say "a resume is used to get a job"?

That's because resumes don't 'get' you a job. YOU get a job through networking, interviewing, and negotiating.

A resume is simply a tool to make that easier.

Now you be saying to yourself that if a resume doesn't get you a job, why do we need one or care about how well they're written?

The simplest answer: Your resume is YOU. It's a stand-in professional biography that, when it is well-written will capture the attention of people who can get you in touch with the sort of job you're looking for. It's a marketing piece that not only showcases your accomplishments and abilities but creates interest.

As is often said in the marketing world: You don't sell the steak, you sell the sizzle. This means essentially that all beef is the same, but to a hungry person, the sensation of steak cooking will capture and hold the imagination. Make people hungry and you'll sell much more steak!

You might ask: how do you write a resume like that when you aren't versed in marketing or writing advertising copy?

The good news is that you're uniquely familiar with the offerings of the business you're selling because that business is you! Using that knowledge, you can follow the steps outlined here to compile all the information you need in a way that serves to present what you've got to offer a potential employer in a way that is relevant and compelling. Once you've laid out your case that you're a good candidate, you've got a better chance to land an interview.

That's really what resumes do: get you in the door so you can convince the hiring managers that you're the best fit for their needs.

To complete the writing process, we've compiled the steps from our resume writing workshops to guide you through the writing process. Each step has a corresponding assignment and will move you further along the way until you've created a resume that wins the interview.

Step #1 you will be introduced to the basic structure of a resume and gather relevant personal information.

Step #2 you will create a properly formatted resume document.

Step #3 you will write the content of the resume in a series of separate exercises.

It is important to keep in mind as you go through these steps is that success is always biased towards action. Be actively engaged in the writing assignments presented at each step. Once they are completed you will have written a resume for yourself which is no small feat! Schedule writing sessions at each step to keep yourself on track. The sooner you start writing, the sooner you'll have a resume. Putting it off until 'later' will decrease your chances of successful completion.

There is no 'I' in 'resume' (resume-speak)

We are often asked this question: Why don't resumes read like 'regular' documents?

That's because resumes are written in <u>1st person without pronouns</u>. (Don't worry if you can't remember what that means from your high school English class.)

In a normal document or conversation when you're referencing something you've done, you would say:

"I led a team of four in the upgrade our ERP system"

But in a resume, you switch to "resume-speak" and say:

"Led a team of four in the upgrade of the ERP system"

What you've done in this example is referred to yourself in the third person ('John led a team…') and then removed your name.

The easiest rule of thumb to follow is: Avoid the use of the word "I" in a resume!

Note about LinkedIn and online profiles.

You should closely mirror your resume and your LinkedIn profile, but you can use 1st person pronouns on your LinkedIn header. While your Summary section might say 'Enterprise administrator with experience in DX" you can choose to have it written on you LinkedIn to say "I am an Enterprise administrator…". This is a personal and aesthetic choice.

Resume pitfalls

Resumes have been around for a long time so chances are good you may have seen some of these before.

We're listing them here so that you do NOT include them.

Lingo and jargon: Not everyone who reads your resume may understand your industry, so write as if you were speaking to someone who doesn't know your line of work.

Buzzwords: You may think 'leverage synergies to optimize potential' sounds like it would belong on your resume, but it does not.

Acronyms without definitions: Spelling out the words to avoid confusion e.g. *Served as Subject Matter Expert (SME) on multiple projects.*

"References available on request": This is assumed, so leave it off the page.

A career or job 'objective': A hiring manager can figure this out from your resume. Also, the resume isn't about what you want, it is about what you can offer the employer.

Subjective descriptions: Anyone can claim to be 'creative', a 'people person', a 'strong leader'. Demonstrate these traits with your accomplishments, don't just make statements without evidence.

Pictures, icons, charts, and other gimmicks: This can be used on a secondary resume (sometimes called an infographic or networking resume) that you hand out to people directly, but don't use them in a professional resume.

Outdated skills and technologies: If your industry does not use technology, software, or system anymore, you do not need it in our document.

Filler or 'fluff' data: Do not waste space with things that are not relevant to the position. One example- hobbies.

"Salary Negotiable": Again, this is assumed.

Unprofessional email addresses: If you want to use beerbrewer73@aol for your personal emails that's fine, but use or create a more professional address at a major email service provider for professional, resume-related correspondence.

For example: jane.doe73@gmail or filastname@outlook

Hallmarks of a good resume

The bad news:

It is very easy to write a bad resume.

The good news:

The effort you put into a good resume pays off!

A good resume has the following attributes:

Easy to read – The average time spent reading a resume is 10-15 seconds, so make it easy to get the important details. Focus on being able to skim the page and draw the eye to important information.

Engaging content – Don't be boring. Try instead to tell a story.

Tells the truth – *Never* lie on a resume.

Designed for ATS (Applicant Tracking System) read-ability– online job boards often reject resumes before a human ever sees them if they're not formatted correctly.

Well-written – proofread and typo-free.

Visually appealing – Clean, modern, and quickly show the relevant information.

Showcases the applicant's accomplishments and value – Tells a story of what you've done, what you can do, and how you can do that for your future employer.

Demonstrates valuable professional qualities – shows leadership, collaboration, adaptability, emotional intelligence, etc.

Uses Action Verbs – Led, Managed, Developed, Built, Processed, etc. You can find examples in the appendix or search online.

Resumes show Accomplishments

A common mistake that resume writers make is to merely recount their job description for the position they held.

Here is an (exaggerated) example:

Floor Supervisor – XYZ Fake Biz Inc 2015-2018

Supervise staff, lift 25 lbs unencumbered, able to stand for long periods, did other duties as assigned

Modern Resumes use Actions Verbs, sometimes called Power Words, to convey not only what was done but what was accomplished.

Here the same example as above, but showing what was accomplished:

Floor Supervisor – XYZ Fake Biz Inc 2015-2018

Led a team of 12 staff, overseeing customer service and product expediting. Provided direct oversight of workplace safety and conditions. Adapted quickly in response to management directives.

Do you see the difference?

In the first example, we are shown the job description and not much else.

In the second example, we learned the person managed a staff of 12, what they did, extra duties the person was responsible for, and their ability to be flexible.

Here's another example:

Account Manager – ABC PseudoCorp 2016 – Present

Sold widgets and managed accounts

The same, with action verbs and metrics:

Account Manager – ABC PseudoCorp 2016 – Present

Managed client accounts to generate 50K widgets sold in the first year and drove 10%+ yearly growth.

In the second example, we see not only more of what was done but also what the person was able to achieve.

The goal of writing accomplishments and backing them up with relevant data/metrics is to show not just what you can do, but to generate interest from future employers and make them ask, "Can this person do this for me?"

Resume keywords

What are keywords?

Keywords are just that - the *key words*!

They are the nouns and adjectives that are used to highlight essential skills or traits that hiring managers, recruiters, applicant tracking systems, and search algorithms are looking for. They are flags to call attention to items you want others to pay attention to.

Think of it this way – if you're looking for a Mexican restaurant in Springfield, Missouri, you would go online to a search engine and type "Mexican restaurant Springfield mo". This tells the search engine you want restaurants, specifically Mexican food restaurants, in the town of Springfield, specifically in Missouri.

Example A: A database administrator looking to work with Oracle databases would include mentions of 'Oracle' in their resume. If they mention MS SQL Server, MySQL, or Mongo databases in addition to Oracle, they'll get noticed for those as well. So if they prefer to NOT work with MySQL even though they know it, they'd leave it off their resume so as not to call attention to it.

Example B: A retail manager who wants to pivot into the field of logistics would include keywords such as "warehouse", "delivery", "expediting", and "inventory" to call attention to experience in those related transferable skills.

Example C: An account manager wanting to move up into a more senior role that involves directing a team would include words such as "leader", "managed", "directed", "team", etc.

Tip 1: Make a list of any technical, industry-specific, or professional skills that you want to be recognized for. Take a look at job postings that interest you and see what words repeat and appear frequently. Keep a list of what you find so you can work them into your resume in both the summary and experience sections.

Tip 2: Skill summary sections are considered standard for technical and engineering resumes, but they don't have to be. You can weave most skills or systems you have experience with into your bullet points and resume content. This saves valuable page real estate!

How a resume is read

Question: On average, how much time do most hiring managers and recruiters spend reading a resume the first time through?

Answer: A few seconds; average is less than 10

A few seconds?!

According to studies, a resume gets very little attention at first glance. So how do you make sure your resume gets MORE than 7 seconds?

You pay attention to these rules of good resume writing.

Keep the layout simple - Simpler is easier to read. Keep it clear and guide the reader where they need to go.

Keep it short and sweet - One page is ideal, two is acceptable, three or more probably means you have cuts to make. Remember to choose quality over quantity.

Avoid too much information - Cluttering the page with every keyword, position, or skill you have is overkill.

Show impact - People want to know you can make change happen and adapt to new situations quickly. The best way to do this is to use metrics and/or data where appropriate.

Focus on accomplishments - By focusing on your professional achievements and projects, you will not have to edit the resume as often.

It's not about you Write about yourself but always keep the reader in mind. What should they know about you and, more importantly, why should they care?

·Write for applying online AND networking Applying to job openings posted online is one strategy to find a job, but it pales in comparison to professional networking. A good resume is useful for both approaches, so keep this in mind as you write. A human and a computer both read this document.

Technical considerations

Before we start writing, let's go over some things that you may encounter as you begin writing your resume in earnest.

File Formats: .DOC, .DOCX, .TXT, .PDF??

There are many file formats to use when writing your resume. Let's review the options and where to use them.

DOCX – This is the modern file format used by Microsoft Word and Google Docs. Your master resume, the one you make all edits from that you are writing, should be in this file format. This file format supports colors, lines, bullets, spacing, and other elements to make it look appealing.

DOC – This is the older file format used by Microsoft Word and is much like the newer DOCX format. DOCX format has replaced it, so choose it instead.

TXT – Also known as a 'text file' or ASCII file, TXT format is the most basic format of a document and removes all the page layout elements. This is useful for being read by an ATS and the file size is very small. If needed, you can always make one from your DOCX file with the 'Save As' option.

PDF – Adobe's Portable Document Format (PDF) is, essentially, a locked-down version of your resume that can not be edited by the reader and looks like it does when printed. This is the version you should share via email and online, but not for uploading to online job applications. You can generate a PDF from Word or DOCs

Pages – A .pages file is created by Apple's Pages app and, while it looks nice, it's often not readable on other machines. If you create a resume in Pages be sure to export as a DOCX file for upload or convert to a PDF before sending it.

Managing your resume file(s)

- *Avoid naming your file just "resume"* While this will work, a more descriptive name will prevent it from getting lost – either with a hiring manager or in your own files. We recommend naming your resume so that it includes your last name, first initial, and then the word 'resume'. So instead of resume.docx it would be FirstInitialLastnameResume.docx. You can also add the year or month/year it was created to track changes.

- ***Make a backup copy of your resume*** This sounds difficult, but it's not. Open your resume and save it again ('save as') as the same file name but with the word backup included (e.g. FirstIntialLastnameResumeBACKUP.docx). Place this file into a subfolder labeled 'backup', then close it. You won't need it again unless you accidentally overwrite your original resume – then you'll be glad you had it

- ***Track your online submissions with* filenames** As you edit your resume to match keywords in job postings, you'll want to make sure you keep track of what changes you've made. To do that, we suggest creating a subfolder with the name of the company you're applying to. Then copy your resume into that folder. Make your edits on that copied document and save it. You'll submit that copy to the job board or attach it to the email. Once you've submitted your application you can add the company name to remind yourself it's been sent. (e.g. FILastnameResumeAmazon.docx)

- ***Email = PDF*** If you email a resume, print/save a PDF version of your resume into the company's subfolder and send that instead of a Docx file. This will ensure that any text formatting does not change. If you are unsure how to generate a PDF file, check your Help section or search online.

Creating a Plain-Text ASCII File (Optional)

Why would you want a text-only (.txt) file copy of your resume? Not only are the file sizes much smaller and easier for ATS scanners to read (or 'parse' in tech-speak) but you can also see for yourself how it would look to a computer system.

A common thing to watch out for is contractions. If you've ever seen a broken headline online you'll recognize that the computer has misread the contraction. This is common, so either avoid contractions in your resume or check your text file to make sure things encode as they should.

Basic Guidelines for Your Resume Document

- **Size:** 8.5×11 Letter/A4
- **Margins:** Use default 1-inch margins. If you need to, you can go to .75 inch margins but this might impact ATS compatibility.
- **Font Size:** 10.5 to 12 point for body text. 14 -16 for title sections
- **Typeface Choice:** There are no hard rules here except that you should stick to common choices found in business documents. Avoid any novel typefaces such as Comic Sans or Papyrus!
- Apple users need to be cautious and choose typefaces available across all platforms as some fonts are Mac exclusive

Typefaces commonly found in resumes include:

- Arial
- Calibri
- Open Sans
- Times New Roman
- Helvetica
- Garamond

Question: "Should a resume be one page or two?"

The answer is "It depends".

We will get into in more detail later but if you CAN get one page of solid information that showcases you quickly and makes an impact- that's the best way to go. For a more seasoned professional, two pages might be necessary and acceptable as long as it is well-written information.

Should you use a resume template?

Microsoft Word and Google Docs both provide a variety of resume templates that make your resume visually appealing even if you're not well-versed in graphic design or page layout.

But should you use them?

If you have mastered Word/Docs, then they can give you a head start, however, most of the template designs are not optimized for being read by a digital system, so there's a chance that using them could result in your resume not getting through an Applicant Tracking System.

Our advice is to write in a traditional format first. After that's completed then you can tackle a more advanced visual layout that you can give directly to others.

Another drawback to using templates: visual appeal is subjective. What you might think is a real winner, another person might regard as a poor attempt. It's better to play it safe and choose a conservative style over a flashy one unless you're a designer and know what works and what doesn't in a visual medium.

In any case, do not use a template-based resume to apply for jobs online. Only use it in a person-to-person scenario.

Refer to Appendix B for a template layout that you can use. It does not contain the elements that might confuse an ATS, so feel free to use it as a guide for your own resume.

Should I avoid online resume generators?

There's a rule of data security that applies to most everything you find online that is free to use:

If it's 'free' you are potentially the product not the consumer.

What does that mean? Simply put when a company offers to help you online for free, you have to consider why they're doing it. Often the site offering to compile your data into a resume or scan your existing resume to see if it is ATS-compatible is making money from that free service in some way. This can be something as benign as showing you advertising on their site, which is usually the case. Sometimes it is less innocent, and your data could be used for other purposes that you inadvertently agreed to.

Our advice: Write your own resume and be a wise consumer online.

What about "infographic resumes"?

We are often asked about infographic resumes – resumes that are designed to be visually appealing and stand out from the rest by using graphic elements such as charts and pictures. We refer to them as "Networking Resumes" because that's what they should be used for- networking.

You can use a graphical resume for person-to-person networking by email, print, or texting. They're also great for use on LinkedIn, Instagram, and other personal web-presences where they can be shared and downloaded. **If** you have a graphical resume created for you or you create one yourself do NOT use them to apply for jobs. Stick to a traditional format.

What is meant by a Page Header and a Resume Header?

In Microsoft Word or Google Docs, a document has an optional space at the top and the bottom of each page called the Page Header and the Page Footer. The Page Header is frequently confused in discussion with your Resume Header where you have your name, email, and phone number.

When writing a resume, you may be tempted to place your Resume Header into the Page Header – you must NEVER do this. It may seem like you're saving space by using it, but it is a bad idea.

Why? Because resumes today are almost always scanned into an Applicant Tracking System (ATS) which do not look at the page header area. This means if you use the Page Header space and upload your resume for a job, the information listed there is not included. So if your name and contact information are in this page header they can get lost and the system might throw your resume out. Worse yet, the hiring manager could get the resume for the perfect candidate but not know their name or how to contact them!

Contents of resume

Let's get writing!

A modern resume breaks down into six distinct sections. These are commonly accepted practices and you should adhere as closely as possible to avoid confusing the reader or search algorithms.

1. Your Resume starts each page with a Header. This contains your name, address, phone number, and may include relevant links (LinkedIn, portfolio, etc.).

2. Professional Summary. A two to three sentence synopsis of your professional characteristics and 'brand narrative'.

3. Key Accomplishments. Select career highlights demonstrating relevant past achievements that would be of interest to future employers.

4. Experience and Employment History. This is a chronological list of jobs going back ten to fifteen years. This information leads with the job title, employer, length of service, a brief summary of the role performed, and more accomplishments specific to that time.

5. Supporting Data and Achievements. These sections bolster your presentation by showcasing Education, Awards, Certifications, Licensure, Volunteer Engagements, and Affiliations.

6. Technical Skills Summary. An optional section that is used to list technical and vocational skills. Serves as a keyword section when this information is not easily included in the narrative of employment history.

Writing Activity #1 - Getting Started

The first step to writing your resume is to collect all of the information that's needed for the document. Think of this as getting all of the ingredients together before preparing to cook a meal. You could try to collect ingredients as you need them but having them all together before you start working makes things go much smoother.

Before you begin tackling the writing assignments, we encourage you to complete this exercise- you will be thankful you did.

The 10 Things You Need: Your Resume Information Checklist

1. **Employment History (Past and Present)**
2. **Key Accomplishments/Projects**
3. **Education Information**
4. **Certification/License Information**
5. **Volunteer and Community Involvement**
6. **Training**
7. **Technical Skills / Platforms**
8. **Awards and Honors**
9. **Things an employer should know about you**
10. **Industry Keywords**

Employment History

- You will want to list the jobs you've had over the last 10-15 years including titles and dates of employment.
- The time frame for relevance of most positions is 10-15 years unless the position in question stretches beyond that. Including your entire employment history can inadvertently cause age-related bias, so focus on your most recent experiences and projects.
- Avoid any experience or projects prior to the year 2000.

Education

- List just your degree, area of study, and institution.

- If you attended without completing a degree you may substitute just the institution name and the word 'coursework' plus your area of study instead of the degree conferred.
- You do not need to include your dates of attendance or graduation – this can be used to identify your age.

Certification/Licensure

- Include any relevant and applicable certifications and/or licenses.
- Reference the issuing institution or company name with each license/certification.

Training

- Relevant training courses within a 5-10 year timeframe are good to add.
- Include who provided the training for internal or external classes.

Technical Skills/Platforms

- This is important for individual contributors or persons in specific professional fields (I.T., HR, Accounting) however when possible try to include any relevant software within your Employment History/Experience.
- If you do include a block of technical skills, be selective, and don't include basic things that can be assumed given your work history.
- Only list current software or platforms and omit expired products.

Awards and Honors

- Include the name of the awards and who granted them.
- Stay within a 5-10 year time frame.

Things an employer would need to know about you

- This will become important as you write your professional summary.

- Think of this as how you might write a professional biography.
- Make note of the demonstrable character traits you would like to be known for.

<u>Keywords</u>

- Every industry has terms and phrases that are specific to the profession, so include them.
- Spell out acronyms for anyone outside your industry who might read your resume. *Never assume the reader knows what you are talking about.*
- If you see certain words and phrases that are consistently appearing in your job searches, try to work them into your resume.

<u>Writing Activity #1</u>

Collect the information listed above and create a document to organize it all.

You will use this later as a source as you write and you can copy/paste the information you collect so you don't have to re-type it.

Writing Activity #2 - Resume Header

This is the easiest part!

At the top of the document, you will place your name, your email address, and your phone number.

First Name Last Name

(XXX) 555.1212 no_reply@domaindotcom

See? Easy!

You can insert a line below it to mark the beginning of the content, but that's completely optional.

You might have some questions here. Traditionally, a resume includes a person's mailing address, doesn't it?

Traditionally yes, but not today. Why? Because hiring managers can consciously or unconsciously use this personal information to determine if the candidate (you) is 'too far away'. Worse yet, they can make assumptions about you personally based on your location. To circumvent this, omit the address.

Also, if you're looking for remote jobs this information is mostly irrelevant.

You may add your region if your current/last company or phone area code don't match your current city. One way to do this is to include the name of the metro or the metro region (e.g. Metro Chicago, Bay Area California, Dallas-Fort Worth, etc.)

Other Header items to consider

Titles/Post-Nominals:

If you have a degree, license, or certification that you wish to use you can certainly add them. You may wish to omit them on resumes uploaded with applications because a computer might misinterpret Dr. John Doe SHRM Ph.D. as First Name = "Dr John" and Last Name as "Doe Shrm Phd".

FIND WORK WORTH DOING

LinkedIn Public Profile URL:

Hiring Managers almost always review your LinkedIn profile in addition to your resume, so make certain they're looking at the correct person. Search your name on LinkedIn and see how many others come up with identical or similar names- you'll probably be amazed. Copying the LinkedIn URL, more commonly called a hyperlink or web address, could be useful. Write it out instead of copy/pasting the link to avoid getting caught in an email filter. (remove the "https://www.")

An example of a LinkedIn URL would be: linkedin.com/in/username

If your URL contains extra random characters, which is frequently the case, LinkedIn allows you to edit your URL. Everyone should consider doing this but it is especially good to do this if you have a common name or many people share your name. Try searching for your name on LinkedIn- you may be surprised how many of "you" are out there!

Portfolio or website links:

If you have a portfolio or website that is relevant to the positions you're applying to, you can add them as well.

Twitter or other social media feeds:

Add them only if you're using your account(s) to share content related to your industry. Audit your posts if you decide to use them and consider removing potentially offensive or questionable posts that would reflect poorly on you as a candidate.

'Remove' web links from your resume document.

Right-click them and remove the hyperlink. Sometimes spam filters will reject attachments containing hyperlinks. Taking away the https:// will often do the same thing.

Don't panic if you find you miss this step, it's not going to completely sink your resume. It's just best to try not to have them.

Wait! What if you need more than one page?

So, if you have a page 2- do you need a header there as well? Yes, you'll want to include your header on all resume pages* on the off chance the pages get separated.

Simply add ' – Page 2' to your Header on the second page. Match the font size on the body for contrast.

For example:

First Name Last Name – Page 2

(XXX) 555.1212 no_reply@domaindotcom

A word on resume length:

Your resume should not be over two pages unless absolutely necessary. If it's more than two pages, consider editing it to focus on the most essential information. Studies have shown most people read only a small portion of the resume's first page and then skip to the end to check supporting information such as education.

Also, having three or more pages does not always reflect well on the candidate. Try to get to the important point quickly within the first or second page. Reserve page 3 and beyond for items that an essential to your field but not commonly found on others such as publications, patents, project lists, and/or speaking engagements.

<u>Writing Assignment #2</u>

- Create a blank document in MS Word or Google Docs that will become your resume.
- Create the resume header (Remember- not the document header section)

Writing Activity #3 - Summary & Accomplishments

Now you're ready to start writing more of the content for your resume. This is the section that takes the most creative muscle. We're going to focus on the 'Top of the Fold' of your resume-Professional Summary and Key Accomplishments. This is the most important part of your document as far as storytelling goes, so the time spent here is well invested!

Tip: You can always write this section in a separate document and copy/paste it into your resume once you're satisfied with the content.

Be sure to save your work as you progress or turn on auto-save if it is disabled

Writing Samples

Below are some examples from professional resumes to give you an idea of what this section should look like.

Summary Example 1:

Results-driven leader known for identifying opportunities to enhance organizational efficiencies while remaining compliant to complex federal guidelines. Self-motivated problem solver possessing a unique ability to implement technology into organizations to enhance efficiency and service without losing the personal touch. Recognized for a clear and direct communication style that ensures things are done right the first time.

Summary Example 2:

Distance learning professional with over a decade of experience creating strategies to solve performance issues and inspire forward movement, cultivating optimism in uncertain times. Applies proven expertise in instructional design, education technology management, corporate training, and coaching to bridge boundaries through trust and find innovative answers to problems. Known for a human-centered design approach focused on effective solutions to difficult problems.

Key Accomplishment Examples

Remember you only need 3-4 examples on your resume document

- Created a risk index model while collaborating with a five-person team to develop systems and processes to measure risk at 15+ international sites. Implemented a quarterly reporting structure that measured and analyzed both cost and quality metrics to preempt poor inspection outcomes.

- Grew start-up agency to manage 400 projects per year with over $3M in annual sales by providing unprecedented levels of professionalism and customer service.

- Directed accounting functions for internal buyout, ensuring a smooth transition to new leadership. Led transfer to new accounting and payroll systems in addition to employee transitions allowing new leadership to "hit the ground running" without a delay.

- Purchased 20-year-old private industrial distribution firm, ultimately growing annual revenue by 200% in 24 months by building a customer-focused sales culture both in person and via web with online sales becoming 70% of revenue within 36 months.

- Led continuous improvement efforts across four facilities resulting in 5M tons of quality aggregates produced and sold annually.

- Increased productivity by 10% without increasing staff hours worked by identifying opportunities to optimize production while improving quality.

- Built team environment that emphasized smart and efficient solutions, increasing company and client savings from $75K to $160M in hard and soft savings.

<u>Writing Activity #3</u>

- Taking the document, you created in Assignment #2, add your Summary and Key Accomplishments to the document.
- Refer to your list of keywords and try to work them into this section. If you can't, don't worry- you can try to add them in either Work Experience or the Supporting Information sections.
- Be sure to save your document!

Writing Activity #4 - Work History

In this section, we will write the 'meat' of your resume- your professional experience. This section is all about what you can do, which you demonstrate by showing what you've done. The intention here is to entice a future employer to want to meet you because they see potential in your record of accomplishments.

Below is an example from a professional resume to give you an idea of what this section should look like.

Remember: This section starts with the most recent or present position and goes back chronologically over the past ten to twelve years.

Business Development and Operations Representative

XYZ Company
2016 – Present

Responsible for business development for the ABCDEFG Division while simultaneously facilitating Six Sigma Performance Improvement training for 150+ staff members annually. Leveraged educational approach with clients and staff members alike, increasing retention internally and externally.

- Collaborated with Six Sigma Master Black Belt to develop tools to assist with analyzing basic data and identify quality improvement opportunities.
- Retained top accounts through educational presentations with C-suite executives, senior leadership, and front-line leaders on the value of the 1234 program resulting in $1.35M in retained business over 10 years.
- Designed messaging, collateral, and branding in collaboration with the marketing team that met the depth and breadth of client needs.

Now let's break this example down:

The title is listed first and in bold typeface followed by the company that is not in bold. Remember, the resume is about you, not the employer, so always highlight your information, not theirs.

Right align the dates of employment of the same line as your title and company name. Do not put the dates in bold.

ProTip: Use the Tab feature in Word or Docs to right-align your dates, not the spacebar. This is called "Flush Right" and you can search online for "Flush Right Tab in Word" or "Flush Right Tab in Docs" to see how to do this.

Follow this with a brief, two-sentence description of the position. This should be a high-level overview of what you do. Imagine explaining what you do to your favorite 90-year-old aunt. Break down the description in a similar manner.

Let's break down the description to see how it is structured:

"Responsible for business development for the ABCDEFG Division while simultaneously facilitating Six Sigma Performance Improvement training for hundreds of staff members annually. Leveraged educational approach with clients and staff members alike, increasing retention internally and externally."

- *What is this person responsible for?* "Business development within the ABCDEFG Division in addition to facilitating Six Sigma Performance Improvement training for staff."
- *What additional responsibilities does the person have?* "They educate staff and clients resulting in increased retention of both groups."
- List your primary responsibilities followed by your additional ones to create the description of the job.

Let's also look at the accomplishment bullet points:

- Under each position list 3-5 accomplishments that highlight what you're most proud of from your time in that position.

- Be sure these accomplishments are different than any of the accomplishments listed in the Key Accomplishment section.
- Follow the same formatting rules as listed in the previous Key Accomplishment section.

<u>Writing Activity #4</u>

Refer to your Checklist and write your Employment History as shown in the examples.

Writing Activity #5 - Supporting Information

So far in this writing process you've introduced yourself to the reader, communicated your value, showcased your accomplishments, and established your reputation. Now we're going to tackle the achievements that set you apart.

This supporting data includes any or all of the following items:

- Education
- Training
- Licensure/Certifications
- Technical Skills
- Volunteer and Community Engagement
- Associations
- You'll only need to include the information that applies to you.

Below are samples of how you'll want to present this information:

EDUCATION

Master of Science in Leadership
Central State Polytech

Bachelor of Arts, Marketing and Music
Anytown College

Certificate in Project Management
Central State Polytech

- Do not include the years you graduated because this can be used to determine your age.
- If you have a bachelor's degree you do not have to list your Associate degree unless it demonstrates knowledge in a subject that you feel is relevant to an employer.
- Write out the title of your degree if space allows (ATS might be set to look for 'Bachelor of Science' instead of 'B.S.)
- Do not use 'bachelors', 'masters', or 'doctorate' when writing the title of your degree. Those are vernacular terms and should be avoided

LICENSURE

Registered Widget Engineer License #8675309
National Widget Board

- Only include license number if required
- Never list license numbers if this is information that should never be shared publicly

CERTIFICATIONS

Six Sigma Black Belt
XYZ Corporation

TRAINING

Banana 6000 Repair Class
Bloom County Community College

Micrasoft SharePint Administration
Contasa Training Inc.

You may consider listing Certifications and Training in conjunction with Education if space is an issue. Adjust the section title accordingly.

Volunteer Experience

Board of Directors - Fort Where Animal Shelter

Vice President, Board of Directors – Whosburg Athletic Association

PTA Member – Harper Valley School System

Volunteer – Whystown Red Cross

- If the role has no title, 'volunteer' is usually sufficient to explain what you did
- No details are needed on each position but be prepared to explain in an interview what you did in each role.
- Dates of service are optional
- Rank in order of responsibility

Special Considerations

No degree

If you, like the majority of Americans, did not finish a post-high school degree but did attend some college, list the area of study followed by "coursework" and the school you attended.

Example:

Business Administration coursework - University of Indianapolis

Be sure to list any additional training courses, certifications, and licenses you have. These become critical to highlight your continued efforts toward advancing your education despite not having a completed degree.

If you do not have any college credits or degree, you can omit the Education section entirely and focus on others such as Certifications or Training.

If you possess a Certificate that was obtained at a college or university, you can list it under education in place of a degree.

Example:

Leadership Certificate – Loyola University

Military Service

First, if you've served in the military, thank you for your service. If your service was more than ten years ago or was/is in the Reserves, create a section titled Military Service following the Experience section. Following the same format we used in the Experience section, list your final rank, branch of the military, and dates of service if you're currently still serving. If you're not still serving, simply list the final rank and branch of the military. On the next line, give the two-sentence description followed by two or three bullet points highlighting what you accomplished during your service. Be sure to write this in 'civilian speak' and remove any/all jargon, abbreviations, etc.

Visa or USCIS Green Card Status

Some clients opt to list their citizenship or work eligibility status at the end of the resume. If you choose to do so, add this (centered) at the very bottom of the resume.

Additional Language Proficiencies

If you speak languages other than English, consider listing them along with your level of fluency. This shows the reader that you have additional experience that may be valuable to them or their customers.

<u>Writing Activity #5</u>

This assignment requires less effort from a wordsmith perspective, but that does not mean it is less important!

- Referring to the data compiled in Activity #1, add your Supporting Information to the last portion of your resume document.

Writing Activity #6 - Finalizing your document

Congratulations! You've completed the writing assignments and are almost ready to upload your resume. Just a few quick things to consider before you do that.

1. Proofread the document
2. Have an 'editor' look it over
3. Backup your document
4. Schedule your revisions

Get ready to launch, we're in the home stretch!

#1 Proofreading

It's just a fact of life that documents contain typos, misspellings, and errors. Resumes are no different, but it is important to fix them as soon as possible! The document you upload to the internet should be as close to perfect as humanly possible. Mistakes happen, but horror stories about hiring managers dumping a resume because they found a typo exists for a reason. Let's not discover if they're true or not.

Here are some handy tips as your proof your resume:

Use the spell and grammar tools in Word/Docs to double-check

They are not always 100% correct, but they can help you discover obvious errors.

Use a spell and grammar checker.

Regardless if it is an online service or the one built-in to your word processor, make certain to run your document through multiple times.

Read your resume aloud

Read each sentence out loud and see if it flows correctly.

Have your computer read your resume aloud

Alternatively, you can use your Windows/Mac Assistive Technology to read your document back to you.

Get a second pair of eyeballs

Get a friend or family member to read it and let you know if they find any errors.

Read it backward

This really focuses the brain to look at the words- it's hard to do but can often work wonders.

#2 Get an Editor

It's a rule of professional writing that every writer needs a good editor. You're often too familiar with the document as the creator to make objective judgments, so consider asking for outside help.

You can ask a friend or family member to give you their opinion

They are the less objective option of those listed here, but they are better than not having an editor at all.

You can ask co-workers past or present to review your document

This is helpful because they know you, your industry, and your background. Of course, if you're looking for a job and don't want to announce it to your boss or co-workers *make certain you are discrete in who you ask.*

You can also enlist a resume writer or career coach to help

This option costs money but is well spent to have a professional opinion of not only your document but also how you are presenting yourself on paper.

A bonus to having an editor- they can also point out mistakes you may have overlooked. Extra proofreading can't hurt

#3 Make backups of your document

We mentioned it before, but it's worth saying again: Make a backup copy! It's a simple step that will save you headaches should anything happen. Duplicate your document and place it somewhere safe.

#4 Schedule your next revisions

Some people go years and never update their resumes. This is shortsighted and costs precious time if you have the opportunity for a promotion or find yourself in need of a new job. Take the time now and schedule a reminder at a future date to update your accomplishments and check your information.

Cover Letters

You can referrer to Appendix C for an example cover letter to help you in creating your own.

There's great debate about cover letters.

- *Should I write one?*
- *Should you include one even if it's not required?*
- *Even if it's required, does anyone actually read it?*

Our answer to all of these questions is **YES!**

Cover letters are still a requirement in many industries and even if a company does not require them, it's a great opportunity to share your story and sneak in a few keywords in the process. The goal of the cover letter is to introduce yourself to the reader.

The cover letter should be a single page document that tells the reader about you including your background, why you're interested in the position, and how you believe you'll benefit the organization.

Your cover letter should not discuss personal details, attempt to be funny, or repeat all of the information from your resume.

Think of the cover letter as the introduction before a speaker is called to the podium.

Keep it brief, calm, and factual while remaining friendly and approachable.

Use the same font and colors from your resume to keep them consistent.

Create a cover letter template that you can customize for each position you're interested in. This will make the cover letter writing process much faster (5 minutes instead of 20+ minutes).

Composing Your Cover Letter

Use a traditional business letter format when creating the cover letter and save the final copy in PDF format. This will allow you to attach the formal cover letter to your email or online application. Another option is to copy and paste the body of the cover letter into the text of your email to the hiring manager.

You may refer to Appendix C for a sample cover letter if you're unfamiliar with a business letter layout.

Cover Letter Header:

In the top left corner of the letter include your name, phone, and email address.

Next, list the date the letter is being submitted.

Finally, include the hiring manager's name, title, and company name. This may require additional research to find the correct hiring manager's name.

> Your Name
>
> Phone #
>
> Email
>
> Month xx, 2020
>
> Hiring Manager Name
>
> Hiring Manager Title
>
> Hiring Manager Company

Cover Letter Body:

Salutation: Do not start the letter with 'Hi', 'Hey', or the just the first name of the hiring manager. Instead, insert the person's full name. Unless you are sure of the hiring managers preferred pronouns, avoid using Mr., Miss, Ms., or Mrs.

Next state the purpose of the letter. In this case, you're expressing your interest in the specific company and the position you're applying for.

Next, include one or two sentences about who you are as a professional. In most cases, these will be similar statements to those in your summary at the beginning of your resume. Let these showcase the big picture of your work. This will allow you to save these into the master copy and avoid updating them each time. If you're relocating to where the company is located, this is a good place to list that information including the date you plan to arrive. Avoid sharing personal information about why you've relocated.

Following this section, include information about the job requirements and how you match them. This can be listed in a bullet point format or in paragraph form. In either case, mention the requirements that you match best and then share accomplishments or specific experiences that demonstrate how you match those requirements. Limit this to three or fewer requirements.

Finally, let the reader know your resume is included and that you appreciate their time.

Example Body:

Mrs. Sally Brown,

I would like to express my interest in Charles Brown and Associates and the position of Kite Designer. As an experienced aeronautics engineer professional, I am known for crafting innovative airframes that are both high-performance and efficient. Below I have outlined how my skills match your requirements for this position. I appreciate your consideration for employment with CB&A

Your Requirement:

Designing Tree-proof lifting bodies

My Qualification:

I was the lead engineer on the Kite 2015 project for Lockheed Martin

Your Requirement:

13 Year progressive experience in engineering design

My Qualification:

Advanced from Junior Engineer to Head of Kite Engineering from 2002 - Present

Your Requirement:

Able to lead to cross-functional team

My Qualification:

Collaborated closely with research team from Van Pelt University over 10-year span

My resume is included for your review. Thank you for taking the time to review my credentials and experience.

Complimentary Close:

Keep this simple and professional. Use 'Sincerely' and sign it with your legal name.

If you have a digital image of your signature, add it above your typed name.

Save the document in DOCX and PDF formats using your first initial, last name, company name, cover letter as the document name. Example: *FNamerson_ABC_Coverletter*

This will tell the reader who the cover letter belongs to and will remind you which company you sent the letter to.

ProTip: Make a Cover Letter Template

You'll want to create a template named FirstInitialLastNameCoverTEMPLATE.docx that you can duplicate and edit for each position you apply to (FILastNameCoverXYZCORP.docx).

You'll be able to easily track your applications by file name if you duplicate the file and edit as needed.

Dealing with Applicant Tracking Systems (ATS)

Your resume is only one item in your job search toolkit. Now you need to make a plan to handle Applicant Tracking Systems.

Each time you submit your documents to a potential employer, chances are good that it will be read by a computer algorithm long before it is ever seen by human eyes. This ATS could decide that you don't meet certain criteria and prevent your resume from going past this point.

Never be afraid of an ATS! We've covered most of the things you need to know to get around them, here's a guide to refer to later on.

All varieties of companies are using Applicant Tracking Systems (ATS) to manage the influx of resumes from online postings. There are numerous reasons why companies use them, and we believe that ATS's will continue to be a fact of life for job seekers today and into the future. Every time you attach a resume to an online job application, there's a better than average chance the first person to read your document isn't a person, but an algorithm. Having a plan to deal with an ATS is vital to success

Much like a bouncer at a fancy night club, the ATS software decides who gets in and who stays outside. This means that you need to design your resume to be able to navigate this gauntlet to get inside to a human reviewer. Here's a series of tips to help you make sure you don't get the heave-ho out the door but instead get invited to the VIP section.

The following are some tips to help you build confidence that your resume is getting past the ATS to a human being for review.

Formatting can trip up the process

You might assume that graphic elements enhance readability. For people that may be the case but computers can't make sense of them. Avoid text boxes, graphics, borders, underlines, and color. Make sure your text is left-aligned with normal margins. Bold text and capitalization are fine. Use lines that are inserted as elements not underlines.

Check things out in plain text

Curious about how your resume reads from the ATS perspective? Try copy/pasting your content in a plain text editor (Windows – Notepad, Mac – Text Editor). If something seems amiss, it could throw off an ATS.

Upload .docx files

Maybe you don't use Microsoft Word to write your resume, but when uploading to an ATS be sure to upload only .docx format. Anything else might not be able to be scanned correctly. PDFs are great for email, but they're not always machine-readable.

Use standard fonts

Never use a font that is smaller than 10 points or larger than 12 for the main text of your document. Header can be 14-16 points to stand out.

Stick to standard resume fonts such as Arial, Calibri, Garamond, Helvetica, and the like. Avoid dramatic typefaces and stick to one for the entire document if you can. Never use more than two different fonts.

Never use the headers/footer space

At the very top and bottom of a digital document there is an area called the 'header' and 'footer'. If you're unsure about what this is, look it up in either the help section or online.

It is important to NEVER use this space because most ATS will never look here. If your name, email, and phone are located here then your resume might be flushed because you have no name.

Spell out acronyms, slang/jargon

Sure, most everyone might know what an MBA or CPA is, but you can't assume that. Master of Business Administration (MBA) makes it better for humans. Either way, if the ATS is looking for CPA or Certified Public Accountant you'll be covered.

Be wary of keyboard symbols

Have you ever seen a headline that should say "Can't" but instead there are random characters instead of the apostrophe? This happens when the system is unable to understand what the character actually is. Avoid contractions if you can, just to be safe. When in doubt, try the trick in Tip #12 to see what happens.

Avoid TMI (Too Much Information)

This applies to both people and computer systems. Your resume will get about 5-10 seconds of attention assuming it makes it past the ATS. Don't bother including information more than 10-15 years old unless it's vitally important. An ATS might throw you out if you have too much data.

Skills sections are both good and bad

Unless you're in a technical field, you might consider dumping a Skills section and instead include your skills with each job. If you have one, place it at the end of the document.

Use standard section headers

The ATS will look for section headers such as Employment, Employment History, Experience, Education, Certification, etc. Creativity is nice just don't do it for section headers.

Don't use Grandpa's 'word salad' tricks

You might be told by some to include all your keywords either in a block of text, a skills section, or (worst of all) white text at the bottom of the page. Systems are a lot smarter than they were when this was a good tactic. Just don't do it.

Finally, remember this rule: *Computers are two things - helpful and stupid.*

ATS systems exist to speed up the job application process but they're only as smart as they are programmed to be. Do not let the idea that an algorithm will read your resume first be a source of stress for you. The system is actively trying to get your resume where it needs to go and keep out the riffraff; it's not trying to hurt your chances of being seen but is actively trying to help you.

Help your chances by making your resume easier for the ATS to read.

ffff fff

Section 5: Career Tactics - Job Search

"The brick walls are there for a reason.

The brick walls are not there to keep us out.

The brick walls are there to show us how badly we want something."

—*Randy Pausch*

Misunderstandings about the job search

Before we go ahead and dive in, let's clear up some myths that just won't seem to go away when it comes to finding a job:

Job Descriptions describe the job in 100% detail.

Sometimes this is true but more often than not a job description posted for an open position describes the ideal candidate. Many fail to apply for jobs they're qualified for because they don't meet every qualification listed.

Any job will do

It's not unusual for career management professionals to make the analogy that job seeking is a lot like dating. You don't want to meet just anyone; you want to meet the right one! Remember, you're interviewing your potential employer as much as they are interviewing you because to truly create value BOTH parties have to be happy.

Skills all at the matter

While this may have been true once, it's far less true now. Of course, for certain technical positions skills are important but by far the most important attribute of a successful candidate is one who can communicate their accomplishments. This reveals much about the candidate's character, style, and professionalism. Taking a job at a place where your skills fit but you personally don't is a recipe for a miserable job and poor performance. Aim to find a place where you are celebrated, not merely tolerated.

Resumes get jobs

Resumes are a tool. Nobody ever hired a resume. YOU get the job. They hire YOU.

Rejection means I'm not qualified

Rejection isn't anything personal. Job seekers need to get used to being comfortable with rejection because it is part of the process. They're not rejecting you personally, they're just saying that you are not the best fit for what they have now. Don't let it get you down, otherwise, you'll find the process so distasteful that you're more willing to stay in at a dead-end than face change. Change is one of the most constant things in human existence and you can short-change yourself and miss opportunities if you're not willing to take a risk for yourself.

My skills are in demand and the market's hot – this won't take long at all

There are no guarantees of success or time that can be offered when you're talking about a job search. You will put in a lot of effort to get your next job. You might think the days of easy jobs are over and you'd be right- but it was never 'easy'. Looking for work is a job in itself.

Your PCI - Personal Career Inventory

Regardless if you're switching careers, looking for another job while employed, or find yourself out of work you always start in the same place – you!

Good news – you know you fairly well.

Bad news – you need to get comfortable looking at yourself objectively (as if you were an outsider). That starts with taking stock in yourself.

Why do you take inventory?

Knowing what you have to work with (skills, experience, accomplishments) and what particular type of employment you're trying to work towards (level, title, salary, location) can help you to set goals and keep a consistent message.

- Set Goals.
- Keep a consistent message.
- Be ready when an opportunity comes along
- Build a system to track your job search

Start with your Toolkit

These are the items you need for a modern job search:

- An accomplishment-focused resume in .docx file format
- A cover letter template
- A personal email account
- A professional headshot
- A LinkedIn account (with a profile that is completely filled out)
- A list of your professional contacts and references
- A system to track tasks- spreadsheet, calendar, app, etc.

Define what you're aiming to achieve

You most likely don't want just any job; you want a job that suits you well. These steps help you find what that looks like.

- Outline your target job(s) - title, level of experience, level of authority, required skills.
- Compensation range - the minimum required and industry average based on market
- Gaps - if you're missing vital experience or level of development then do you need to close them first?
- Geographic location – Also factor the cost of a commute into future compensation goals.
- Remote options - Work from the office or anywhere?
- Benefits – benefits factor into the total compensation package. A lower-paying job might actually pay more once you consider the benefits package.

Your Value Proposition

Hiring anyone costs money and takes risk, so knowing this helps you showcase what you bring to a potential employer and why you are worth being hired.

- Work experience
- Education
- Training and certification
- Demonstrated accomplishments
- Technical skills
- Relevant volunteer work
- Awards and recognitions

Your value as a candidate is best summed up by answering this question: ***What problem can you solve for an employer?***

Planning your search

"Plan your work and work your plan"

You've gone through all the steps of a Personal Career Inventory, what do you do next?

- Organize your network – Everyone has a network of people they know. Chances are good you'll have an easier time getting a new position if reach you out and connect with others who might be able to help you. Learning how to properly network is a valuable investment in personal development.
- Outline your commitment – set a goal for how many resumes you'll send a week, how many jobs you'll apply for, and how many people you'll connect with.
- Get Organized – Create folders on your computer to save copies of each cover letter you send. Have your resume, cover letter, and references in an easy to find location.
- Make a backup of your resume – if you ever edit it to change keywords, etc. you'll want to have a backup copy just in case.
- Set a reminder – set a reminder to log in each day and check for new job postings and apply. Finding a new job is full-time work, so the best way to increase your odds is to spend time daily working to find a job.
- Log your work – keep a journal or spreadsheet of where you applied and what actions you have taken so you can refer to it later.
- Schedule your follow-ups – this is important when you're following job openings that come from networking or direct connections. Don't forget to follow up (just not so much that you become a pest)
- Create email rules – this is optional but helpful. Create folders and email rules to organize your incoming job alerts.
- Print your value proposition statement and keep it where you can see it – the more effort you put into memorizing it, the more focused you'll be.
- Get the app – If you have a smartphone or tablet, consider installing the LinkedIn app and the app of any job board you

use. You can access them easier that way when you're away from your computer or laptop.

- Create an email draft with your resume attached – this allows you to quickly send it to anyone who requests it.

Your social media plan

What is a 'personal brand'?

There are many possible answers, but in career management all boils down to your reputation. While you can't control what people say and think about you, you can control how you present yourself and that is the key to building an image and telling a story in social media circles (and beyond). To achieve results, it is helpful when social media consistently represents the professional image you want to present online. It should reflect the best parts of your present and past work and establish as your reputation - which is what a 'personal brand' truly is.

Most job seekers want that message to be:

- *Hire Me!*
- *Work with Me!*
- *I'm a professional!*

Ask yourself- does my online activity and content send that message?

Where do you start?

Start by assessing the social media landscape and figuring out how you fit in.

Who Am I Online? Where do I have accounts? This is the easiest step – where are you online? Do you spend a lot of time there? Look at your profiles and determine what your activity and content say about you. To a stranger, you ARE the sum of your online profiles and activity.

What do my actions/information say about me? This one is a little harder. Are you political online? Religious? Sports fan? Every share, like, tweet, comment, photo, or piece of original content makes a statement. We've all seen stories of a person who runs afoul of their employer for something said online. Understand that your social media activity is NOT private and has a real-life impact on you and your professional reputation.

What do I think others might say about me? Be empathetic and put yourself in your intended audience (future employers) shoes. Look at yourself objectively and see what you would think about you if you didn't know you. This is a little harder and it can be helpful to have a trusted friend give you feedback.

What can I say differently to make what I want to say clearer? Review your recent content and traffic- is it resonating with the right people? You will want to balance being authentic, consistent, and intentional with being timely and honest. This can be a tricky balance to find but it's worth the effort.

Where is my audience? Finding the people that you want to connect to can be the hardest of all. There's sometimes no way of knowing beyond trial-and-error if you're getting the attention you want. This takes risk, determination, and discipline to get right and you won't always get it right the first time. Do NOT give up on this but by all means pivot and change until you get it right.

LinkedIn is KING!

As far as social media for your career is concerned, there is only one king and that's LinkedIn. Unlike the other social networks out there, LinkedIn focuses on your professional life and creating connections (aka 'networking) with other professionals you know and want to know. It is the first place that career seekers should go to start and if you've already got an account, great! If you don't, then getting one ASAP.

About Facebook, Twitter, Instagram, etc.

What about Facebook, Twitter, Instagram, Snapchat, etc? When it comes to other social networks, they have two roles in the professional job search: brand building and research.

From a brand and reputation standpoint, most social networks are only visible to outside parties if you choose your profile data to be publicly accessible. If you lock down your profile, you restrict your branding to your circle of social media friends and followers. This might seem it's airtight but sometimes it's not as secure as it seems. Social Media platforms WANT you to be as public as possible often times because that creates social friction which creates views which drives advertising revenue. Twitter is one example – tweets are public by default. They need people shouting into the Twitterverse. The dirty little secret of all social media is you frequently don't know who's watching you. The professional reputation you build on LinkedIn could be undone if your clients or future employer find you on other networks and you're a dumpster fire of toxic content. It's important to note here that on social media 'toxic' is in the eye of the beholder!

Bottom line: The content you create and share is what will establish your reputation. Don't blow your chances of landing a new job by posting the wrong thing online.

Create Content

When you think of 'creating content' for social media you might assume that we're talking about people who make videos, graphics, blog posts, etc.

Technically speaking, and for career management purposes, EVERYONE creates social media content. You create content when you:

- Comment
- Share an article
- Upload a picture
- Almost ANY interaction that generates a traceable action that points back to you is a form of content creation because it leaves breadcrumbs back to your message.

Do you think nobody's reading your stuff online? They most certainly are! The platform is counting on it.

When you do share:

Intentionally decide on the audience by focusing on content that makes a statement about who you are (this happens by default anyway). An easy way to do this is to think before posting anything 'what would my boss/future boss think of this?' and with that in mind ask 'Am I going to regret this later?'

Is this a turning social media into a complete buzzkill? Perhaps a little. But if you're seeking a new job you need to be mindful that what you consider 'authenticity' another person might consider as a mark that means you're not the best candidate.

So why not just STOP all social media posting?

You could do that, but you'll run afoul of another problem: if you don't exist online you might lose out to someone who DOES.

Think of it like this:

1. Candidate A has no social media presence.
2. Candidates B and C have social media.
3. Candidate B posts many things publicly that reflect poorly on their character.
4. Candidate C posts things that showcase them as a good person to work with.

Now if you were an employer *and you received resumes from these candidates, but only had one opening, which candidate are you more likely to form a positive opinion about quickly?*

The answer is Candidate C - they are the easiest to find and they put in effort to look their best.

Don't believe it? How often do you use a search engine to find a restaurant or business? So why should you think that potential employers going to be any different? It's a human response.

What should you do for a content plan?

As a rule of thumb, try to post a unique insight, a useful comment (useful, not just 'I agree'), a helpful question, or an interaction (a 'like') on the platform you choose at least once a day, 5 days a week.

It's the bare minimum, of course, try to do more if you can. This is just enough activity to show the social media algorithms that you're still active.

How to be seen in a crowded social media room

You may have heard of SEO – Search Engine Optimization. It's a web design principle that focuses on making sure the content on a website is easily found when a search engine scans it. If an outdoor clothing site has SEO designed correctly, they'll show up higher in the search ranks to the right people who search for 'outdoor clothing'. If they were to be optimized for just 'clothing' and not 'outdoor clothing' then they might show up to people looking for formalwear or business suits.

Personal SEO is like that because you're positioning your profile to be found by the right clients for the right reasons. If you're an accountant in Omaha looking for similar jobs, you want to show up in searches for 'accountant in Omaha' and not searches for 'plumbers in Tulsa'.

1.Your Name.

Here's an experiment. Log onto LinkedIn and type in your name. Count how many people show up. LinkedIn is more than a social media platform, it's a search engine.

Now search 'James Smith' – you'll find a lot and if you happen to be a James Smith who goes by 'Jim Smith' you might find yourself fighting to be found by people who get your resume and want to learn more about you.

2. What you're known for.

Personal SEO doesn't just impact those finding you by name. It also impacts users trying to find you by skill. On LinkedIn and most job boards like Indeed, Monster, etc. a person's profile is marked with certain keywords, on LinkedIn they're called 'skills'. Recruiters will search the candidate pool by geography and skill to find candidates they might want to contact. So if your keyword skill lists 'cisco switches', 'HP servers', and 'python' as your 3 top skills then when a recruiter goes looking for someone with those skills you will be towards the top of that list.

3. Where you are.

This is fairly self-explanatory. Your location matters, so make sure that if you live in a major metro list that as your location instead of the specific suburb you live in.

4. What you build

This is for people who make personally branded content for online use. If you blog or vlog, regardless of the topic you are increasing your Personal SEO assuming your name is attached to your work. This is a good reason to keep your content cross-posted on a personal website or blog and not just the major social media platforms.

Online job search

You have your Resume.

You have your LinkedIn profile.

You've got your social media secured and cleaned up.

Now, where do you FIND the job you want?

Welcome to your new temp job: Job Detective.

As we talked about earlier, job searching used to be a "simple" matter of finding an opening you're a good fit for and applying to it.

First, let's talk about public job openings.

There are 3 general places you'll find public job openings:

1. *Job boards*
2. *Websites*
3. *Search engines*

[The internet is always changing, and as of the publication date, this information is current. As things change though you'll need to be ready to adapt as this information changes. We're teaching you how to fish here, not the exact spot to cast your line]

Job Boards

Job boards sometimes called job aggregators, are the place that most people go to start their job search. It should be yours as well because there is a wealth of jobs that need to be filled there. However, it is vitally important you don't make it your only source for job leads!

Why?

Because the vast majority of jobs that get filled do NOT come from posted openings. (more on that later)

There are multiple boards to consider, but we're going to focus on the major ones.

LinkedIn Jobs - Yes, LinkedIn is more than a professional social network, it's a place that recruiters and HR staff go to post jobs and find candidates. Your profile on LinkedIn doubles as your resume, so it should contain everything necessary to convey what you've accomplished. The reason we rank it #1 is that you're already there! Sometimes you can even apply with just your profile.

Indeed – The current reigning champion as far as job sites go. You have the ability to set up custom alerts to let you know when jobs that match your criteria become available.

Glassdoor – The great thing about Glassdoor beyond the job feature is that you can see what others think about working at the company. These reviews give you valuable insights into the inner workings of an organization (and help you decide if you want to work there)

ZipRecruiter – An up-and-coming resource because it's business-friendly.

LinkUp and SimplyHired – Two lesser-known resources for jobs with up-to-date listings.

Monster and CareerBuilder – Once considered the top dogs, but now some regard them as the second tier. Do not discount them though!

Facebook Jobs – Check out the pages of companies you're researching or just browse what is in your area.

You might also consider specialized job boards. This is by no means an exhaustive list, there are many like them for major verticals. Do some research on your industry. Here are a few examples:

USAJobs.gov – the official jobs website of the US government.

Dice – Technology Jobs

WeWorkRemotely, FlexJobs, and VirutalVocations – Online and remote job options for those with geographic limitations but good internet access.

The Ladders – for $100K+ jobs

<u>Idealist.org</u> – Nonprofit openings for those who want to do good in their careers.

Moe online resources to consider that can be overlooked:

<u>Alumni job boards</u> – These are not usually accessible to the general public, however, if you're an alumnus of a college or university their career services office might have job posts that you can access.

<u>Recruiting / Staffing Agency sites</u>. For more technical and staff positions, your local staffing agency is a good place to visit. RobertHalf.com is an exceptional resource for technical jobs in this category.

<u>State and local job agencies</u>. Leave no stone unturned!

Company Websites

Job posts often cost money, so companies will often only post on their websites. Even though they're public, they can also be considered 'hidden' jobs because unless you look you might never find them. If you're looking for a job in a specific geographic area, start by listing the employers that you might want to work with and visit their websites. Often, they will have a link directly on their main page for open positions, frequently this is also placed on the 'About Us' or 'Contact Us' menu. Dig a little deeper to find their HR subpage if you have to.'

If you're uncertain what employers might be a good fit, visit the local business journals and chambers of commerce to find out what businesses are in the area you're looking at. At a state-wide level, there are often 'Best Places to Work' rankings that might direct you to companies that are not only hiring but also great places to work.

Search Engines

Let's be honest, we might say search engines but we mostly mean Google. You can use DuckDuckGo, Bing, or other alternatives though. Searching for jobs on Google is an often-overlooked resource for seekers. The drawback is that unlike job boards you can't apply with an already uploaded resume, you have to click through to the actual job posting and apply directly on the company's site. This is sometimes the case with job boards though, so don't let this extra step get you down.

But what and how do you search on Google? On job boards, the search criteria are often spelled out for you. (pick a city, region, and level of job, etc). Google takes a little extra effort, but don't worry it's not as difficult as it sounds.

Boolean Search

To get the most out of Google you're going to have to do what is commonly called a Boolean search. It's the backbone of all search results on the Internet, even if you don't see it. In simplest terms Boolean logic allows you to search for specific words using terms that the search engine can understand (called 'operators')

An important thing to note about Boolean search:

LinkedIn and Google both apply Boolean logic a little differently, so be certain to check out the rules for each before you start. This is just a very basic overview of how it works- do your homework to learn more should you decide to use this (powerful) option.

General Boolean Tips:

You can combine or exclude based with the operators AND, NOT, and OR

- Michigan AND Engineer Jobs
- Jobs Detroit NOT Grand Rapids
- Jobs Denver OR Boulder

You can also use quotation marks to find an exact Phrase:

- "Senior Vice President of Marketing"
- "Mechanical Engineer"
- "IT Manager"

"IT Manager" will return results for that list 'IT Manager' and without them, it will search for both 'it' and 'manager', so results would be for any jobs that say manager in the post. You will not get results for Information Technology Manager though- that would be "Information Technology Manager"

You can use parenthesis to combine modifiers:

- "Agricultural Manager" AND (Dallas NOT Fort Worth)
- Florida Medical Job AND (Jacksonville OR Orlando)

Keywords

Job Research & Keywords

As you search, you will discover one thing very quickly: there are A LOT of jobs out there. Each job you find, however, is more than just a potential new position. It's a goldmine of **KEYWORDS.**

Keywords are phrases and words that hiring managers and job posters use to identify potential candidates. So each job post you come across, even if it's not a good fit, should be read to find out what common phrases come up.

For example, if you see the phrase 'cross-functional' appearing multiple times in numerous posts then it's an industry keyword. If there is a product or platform you have used that shows up multiple times, it's a professional keyword.

Why should you care? Because when internal and external recruiters search for candidates or review your resume/profile they might be looking for these keywords. Make certain to include them.

Example: A recruiter is looking for someone with experience in SalesForce and customer experience. If you have both of those keywords in your profile, the recruiter has a far better chance of finding you than not. Additionally, if you apply for a position that lists both those keywords, the Applicant Tracking System (ATS) will probably put you to the top of the list if those keywords are present.

You can also use these keywords in your online searches, add to your LinkedIn profile, and use them on your resume. Remember, you don't have to have ALL of them, just the most common ones for your industry that a recruiter would be looking for.

A word on 'hidden' jobs and networking

You may have heard or read that not all jobs that are open are posted publicly.

This is *true*.

There is a multitude of reasons why an employer might not want to broadcast a job opening.

- The position might currently be filled by someone (who's getting the axe).
- Having a lot of open jobs might send the wrong signals to their industry.
- HR might not want to pay for an online listing.
- It might be on the website and they want people to find it.
- They're not ready to fill it, but they're open if the right person comes along.
- They don't have full approval from their board of directors.
- They haven't gotten around to posting it yet.
- They don't have to post, they naturally attract the talent they need.

The bottom line is that the only way to find them is to uncover them by connecting with people who know about them.

That's right- the best and only way to find 'hidden' jobs is to **NETWORK**.

By some estimates over 80% of jobs are found through networking, not through applications to a position.

Why is that? Because hiring someone is a risky and expensive proposition from a viewpoint of the employer and people who are referred from a trusted source have a higher rate of return on the investment.

So get ready to go beyond applying for jobs and PROACTIVELY start making professional connections that will build your network. That is the secret to hidden jobs- they are available to trusted colleagues, not the public.

Your resume, LinkedIn profile, cover letter, and search strategy are all tools in your career marketing campaign. Networking is the next tool you need to add. The work you've done so far builds the foundation you need to truly succeed in the networking game.

You might say you don't have a network? That's not entirely true- we all know people both personally and professionally. You will have let them know that you're looking (publicly or in secret) and lead with an offer to help them.

- Friends, colleagues, past co-workers, people you know from school, social connections- all of them can help you!
- You can also investigate potential companies by connecting with people on the inside. Explain you're interested in learning more. Even if you never get a job, you gained experience, knowledge, and made a connection.
- Connect on LinkedIn- that's its main feature after all.
- Volunteer! Joining a new organization or civic group can help you make connections and you get the satisfaction of helping advance a cause.
- Professional organizations, both local and national, exist not just to promote a profession or industry but often help fill open spots for their member organizations.

These person-to-person connections might just lead you to your next position. How does all this work? Human beings like to be helpful. Help others and let them help you.

Your job search - some parting thoughts

Now that you know what it takes to find a job online you might be asking yourself: "Where do I go next?"

The simplest answer is to get to work! Your new 'job' as a detective helps you find jobs but it's up to you do the footwork too.

Take these final tips with you as you get started, they'll help you along the way:

- The more effort you apply to the search, the more likely you'll find results.
- Keep adjusting until you find a way that works for you, just don't quit.
- Don't fear rejection- it's a reality of the job market. Nobody likes it but it's not personal.
- Instead of looking for your 'dream job' look instead for the dream IN the job – focus on how you do your best work and look for ways to do that.
- Lead with an offer, not an ask - To get help, start by giving help
- Network! – you'll find the search process easier because you have people working with you. Be seen in the right place - it can do wonders for your chances of getting a job offer.

Section 6: Career Tactics – Interviewing

"If opportunity doesn't knock, build a door."

–Milton Berle

How to ace the interview

Interviewing for a job seems to be something that most people hate or tolerate. Few people, if anyone, seems to actually enjoy the process. This is understandable because most human beings are uncomfortable being placed in the spotlight and being asked questions about themselves. The act of being interviewed can trigger a deep evolutionary defense response that makes us want to flee the situation. The terror of being scrutinized keeps many people locked into jobs they hate simply because the dull pain of a slow death beats facing the fear of being judged as lacking.

It does not need to be that way though. Ask a salesperson about the first time they made a cold call or ask an actor about the first time they stood on stage. Chances are good they will describe the need to throw up and perfuse sweating. How they did get over it? They got over it by choosing to put their goals over their fears. With preparation and practice, the ability to come face-to-face with another person in an interview scenario becomes easier.

If you've got the courage to look for a new job, don't let the fear of the interview hold you back. You've committed time and effort into writing your resume, searching for the right job, and networking with the right people so don't let this part trip you up. The interview improves your chances of getting the job. It's not the deciding factor, but a good interview balances the odds in your favor.

Preparation phase

Vince Lombardi once said "The will to win is not nearly so important as the will to prepare to win." This is as true in your career as it is in sports. You must be willing to take the steps necessary to train yourself and prepare yourself for the tasks ahead if you hope to achieve the outcome you desire. Getting prepared for an interview is no different.

Let's assume you've gotten an interview with a potential employer. What are the steps you need to follow?

Background Research

The company you're interviewing with wants to know more about you, and you should be in the same mindset. Hiring is more than just a transaction, it's a determination not just that you're a good fit for the company but that the position fits in with your goals and work style. Spend time doing background research through online search engines and the company website learning about:

- Company missions and strategic plans
- Your interviewers' backgrounds and roles
- News about the company
- Who their main clients are?
- Who their leadership is?
- Overall financial health

This process will not only give you insight into what you're possible signing onto but can help you understand how you can best address the problems they need you to solve. It can give you questions that you can bring up later in the interview showing that you've committed to learning about them.

Get Organized

Treat this interview like any business meeting, be prepared to take notes. These notes will best be done in an analog fashion, that's right pen and paper. The reason analog beats electronic is that you won't be distracted by your digital devices during the interview. Even if you do have your phone on your person be sure it's in airplane mode and stored in your pocket.

Items should you take with you to an in-person interview include

- 2 good pens (1 + 1 spare)
- a crisp notebook/padfolio
- the questions you have for them (more on that later)
- the interviewer contact information, location directions (printed)
- enough resumes and printed references for the people you're scheduled to meet with plus at least 2 extra copies.

Having a pen and paper is handy to have for distance interviews too, so keep one close by.

Dress the Part

Unless stated that the interview dress is business casual, always assume that the dress code is business professional. It is preferred to be overdressed than underdressed in these cases. Body language and posture also are important, so don't slouch. Present yourself in the best light possible.

Know What You're Offering

A lot has been written about the elevator pitch, that mythical 20 seconds you have to summarize what you're trying to achieve. While you don't necessarily need to have a perfect answer to the question you should at the very least understand what you're offering in exchange for the job. You can use the standard headline formula found online:

"I do X for Y clients results in Z transformation"

Social Media Audit

This is important to do in any case- check your use of social media. This might mean you set your posts on FB, Twitter, etc. so they're not public. If they are or you have mutual friends that might allow an interviewer to see them, avoid controversial posts. Remember that controversial is a matter of personal taste so stick to dinner table rules and ditch posting about politics, religion, or social issues.

References

Have your references ready in printed form or email draft. Aim to have at least 3 – 1 former direct supervisor, 1 former/current co-worker, 1 former direct report or a personal reference.

Supplemental Materials

If required or requested, be ready to provide your portfolio, proof of certification, etc. Ask the person coordinating the interview if you are required or can bring what you need that helps make your case.

Questions for the interviewer about the position and organization

Print them out and have them handy. We'll discuss our top 10 questions in a later section.

Interview questions you may encounter

There are a few stock questions that tend to appear in every job interview. It is better to think about the answers to them before you encounter them so you're not struggling for an answer. The key with patent questions and answers is to appear that your responses appear spontaneous and not rehearsed.

Important Note: Preparing for these questions, even if you don't encounter them will give you a sense of confidence going into the interview. Before your interview try writing them out or speaking to yourself in the mirror- whatever it takes to get these answers out of your head and into the world.

1. *"Tell me about yourself?"*

This is where you should be able to communicate your value – what you can do and why it's relevant to the employer. Think of this as your "elevator pitch". Keep it to your professional experience and avoid sharing personal details when answering this question.

2. *"What was your biggest success?"*

This question is about finding out how a candidate thinks and performs. Showcase one or two examples of how you used sound judgment, went beyond the call of duty, achieved better-than-expected results, and/or adapted to changing situations.

3. "What was your biggest failure?"

This isn't the 'gotcha' question that it seems. This one is about seeing how you take ownership of the inevitable failure or unintended consequences we all face in life and the workplace specifically. Go beyond owning the failure to showing how you recovered from it and, this is the key to turning the question around, how you learned something from it. It is often said that when you learn from failure, you never truly fail.

4. "Why did you leave X?"

Be honest as to why you left a position, but if there are issues you had at your former employer don't place blame on anyone. Even if they were the worst place to work in the history of employment, nobody needs to know that in an interview. You don't have to be evasive, but also don't bad mouth a former employer.

5. "Why are you looking/what are looking for?"

Use this an opening to talk about the mission of your career. Sharing your vision of what you're trying to do in the world gives an employer the sense that you're looking for more than just getting on their payroll and benefit plan.

6. "Why do you want to work here?"

Assuming you researched the company before the interview (which you should!) you need to talk about where you see the company going and how you can contribute. This question is about them more than it is about you.

7. Questions about qualifications

When you wrote your cover letter you aligned your qualifications and skills with the ones listed in the opening. Be ready to defend your skill level and explain your prior experience. You may also encounter needs the employer has that weren't listed in the job posting so don't panic if they come up, just be honest about what you can do.

In some technical and skills-based positions you may be asked to demonstrate your ability to handle a required task. This is used to screen out who actually can do the work and who can't.

8. Questions about skill gaps

Your resume might make an interviewer question gaps they perceive in your abilities. This isn't personal and not a point for argument but is a time to talk about transferable or adjacent skills that will help you learn these skills. A candidate rarely fits all the criteria perfectly, so be ready to tell them how you've learned and adjusted to new challenges in the past.

9. 'Weird' or rapid-fire questions

Be ready to think on your feet! Interviewers will sometimes use what seem like unrelated questions such as "if you were a sandwich, what sort of sandwich would you be" or puzzles like "How do you measure the height of a tree" to ascertain how a candidate solves problems, thinks abstractly, or responds under pressure. There is little you can do to prepare for them, but you can be ready and not be surprised when they happen.

10. Off-limits or illegal questions

If an employer asks about some legally defined off-limits items, you do not have to answer them. What are they? It varies, some are federal law and some are state-level, and laws are ever-changing so please do your research beforehand by searching online for illegal interview questions or a similar search string to get the most current and relevant data. Search for both national laws and for those that are current for your state/province/territory.

If you do encounter any off-limits questions be prepared to address them with a polite decline.

Off-limit questions may include:

- Marital Status
- Criminal Record
- Religion
- Military Discharge Type
- Children
- Country of Origin
- Personal Debt
- Drug Use
- Age
- Sexual Orientation/Gender Identification
- Current Compensation

The S.T.A.R. Method

A common type of interview you may encounter is a behavioral interview – frequently they are used to allow a candidate to answer questions that explain how they work and what they've done. If you've ever been asked an interview question that starts with something akin to "tell me about a time when…" then you have dealt with behavioral interview questions.

The preferred way to answering questions of this type is using what is called the STAR method or structure for answering questions. Knowing how this method works will prepare you to tell a story in a way that's universally understood. It's also an effective way to tell a story about how you accomplished something in the past.

The acronym 'STAR' stands for

Situation – Task – Action – Result

Situation: Describe the situation (specific and real) that you faced.

Task: Share what needs to be done, the goal, or outcome you were aiming for.

Action: How you went about solving the problem or achieving the objective.

Result: How things turned out in the end explaining what was learned along the way.

Example of STAR questions:

"Describe a situation where you were able to successfully convince a client they were making a bad choice"

"Give an example of a time you effectively analyzed and solved a problem"

"Share how you've dealt with interpersonal conflict in the past?"

"Tell me about a time you presented in front of a large audience"

"Discuss an important marketing campaign you worked on"

"Give an example where you responded coolly under pressure"

"Describe a time you were forced to fire someone you held in high esteem"

"Give an example of how you motivated others"

"Tell me how your ability to research has helped you"

Example of a STAR answer:

"A client had their primary, local email server hardware go down and they were unable to communicate with clients. They needed to get back into service as quickly as possible with minimal loss of data or productivity. My team was able to restore temporary service and redirect mail flow to another virtual server we created in the cloud. We then were able to restore their primary server to working order and used the server we installed as a secondary, failover server so they would be able to avoid complete outages in the future."

"A major donor for our nonprofit decided they would cease funding our mission. I was assigned to court new donors to make up for the 20% drop in income. I created new promotional materials and activated my community network targeting new donors and previous donors who had not contributed recently. Through my efforts, we not only covered the loss but saw a 14% increase in funding by the next fiscal quarter."

STAR should also be your go-to methodology for answering questions

Did you notice something in both the questions and answers? They're invitations and responses to tell a story. Storytelling is what your interview is all about- showing how you're worked in the past and how your abilities can be useful to your potential employer.

Interview locations

Traditionally, interviews only took place in person but now there are many more options available to hiring managers. Each one has some unique challenges, so here are some tips to consider that might help you best prepare for each scenario.

Regardless of location type, always remember these things:

- Be on time. Follow the rule "early is on time / on time is late"
- Be prepared
- Introduce yourself well
- Say "Thank You"
- Get a good sleep the night before
- Hydrate – you'll sound better
- Visit the restroom before the meeting

In-Person Interviews:

Much like a business meeting, you are required to show up to a location and present your case directly. Sometimes they may involve sharing lunch or going for coffee. Refer to our previous checklist and have extra resumes, your portfolio, pens, etc.

Video Interviews:

Similar to in-person because you can read a person's expressions and body language, teleconference software interviews are becoming more commonplace for initial interviews as workforces become more dispersed.

Items to consider with video interviews:

- Be professionally dressed for a video interview.
- Check your background – be neat, tidy, and remove distractions (like clocks)
- Test your computer hardware before to make sure audio and video are working
- Have a solid internet connection

- Tell anyone else in the house to no disturb you during this meeting
- Keep your pets off your call
- Treat this interview as you would a face-to-face
- Close any notification producing apps or software such as email or SMS

Telephone Interviews

These are quickly becoming the initial interview style of choice for first interviews or screening interviews.

Items to consider with phone interviews:

- Make sure your phone is fully charged
- Speak clearly
- A microphone/headset combo allows you to take notes and improves how you sound
- Minimize all distractions
- If possible, talk to yourself in a mirror (not the bathroom mirror) or turn on your computer's camera – your expression comes through in how you speak.

Informational Interviews and Career Fairs

Informational interviews are a unique way to gain knowledge about a potential employer that you want to work with. In an informational interview, you coordinate with a person inside a target company with knowledge of the position you're looking for. When you meet, they are able to review your background and you can ask questions about the internal culture and operations of an organization. Remember when we talked about networking earlier, this is it.

Career Fairs are no longer just for college undergrads and alumni but are hosted by numerous civic and non-profit groups. If an interview is like a blind date, career fairs are like speed dating- you will meet with internal recruiters actively looking to fill roles inside their companies. While this can be hit-or-miss as far as results are concerned, it is often worth the effort because of the networking opportunity.

Treat a Career Fair like a real face-to-face interview and professionally prepare yourself in the same way. Since you'll be meeting a lot of new people consider sending yourself an email with your resume attached that you can forward to someone who asks for your information- you'll capture their email in return. Don't forget to remove the 'FW' from the email subject line.

Why would a job seeker consider these two avenues if they're not offering a job that meets the seeker's criteria? Because even if you're not a good fit today, you might be in the future, so having a connection at a company is a plus. The best way to get a job is almost always through networking and these two avenues can be worth the investment of your time.

More interview types

Case Study Interviews

Case study interviews will present an interviewee with a hypothetical or real-life scenario that aligns with the work functions of the position. You will be judged based on how well you handle the situation and your approach to finding a solution. Be willing to share your thought process – they want you to 'think out loud'.

Group Interviews

Sometimes an open position will be in high demand and an organization may bring in multiple candidates and interview them in a group either through a group project or other group interaction. The goal is to determine how a person responds in a social dynamic.

It's important to note though that the phrase 'group interview' might also refer to a Panel Interview, so be certain to clarify how things will go down when you coordinate with the hiring team.

Panel or Team Interviews

Sometimes you will be interviewed by a group of people in a Panel or Team format. This team can consist of internal staff who interface with the person or the potential future co-workers/managers. When you're asked a question, you'll want to be certain to address the person who asked it while also addressing the others on the panel.

Technical Interviews

This is fairly self-explanatory. Be ready to demonstrate your technical abilities before the interviewer(s).

Questions you need to ask

Interviewing isn't an interrogation where the candidate is grilled for information then sent on their way. No, it's a conversation between two potential partners. You need to determine if the potential employer is a good fit for your needs just as much as you are for theirs. This is a crucial perspective often overlooked if you take a strictly transactional view of the employer-employee relationship. You spend a large portion of time at your job so finding the right fit is something you should strive for because it will improve your job performance and safeguard your peace of mind.

Here is a list of questions you will want to ask during an interview. Notice how they all start with 'what'? This is a rhetorical trick used to trigger the imagination and not the reactive/defensive parts of the brain. Framing your questions with a 'what' at the beginning will assist you in building a rapport during your meeting.

This list is by no means exhaustive, feel free to add and subtract as you see fit. Just remember to print out the questions and take them with you to the interview so you don't forget them.

"What does a successful candidate look like?"

"What are you looking to improve through this role?"

"What does your ideal candidate look like?"

"What are the clients like?"

"What are the goals you want to achieve with this position?"

"What contribution does the position make to the organization?"

"What does success in the position look like?"

"What does a typical day look like?"

"What challenges are you trying to solve?'

"What is workplace culture like?"

"What is the best part of working here?"

ProTip: Before you head out for an interview, write down any specific questions you personally have for the interviewer so you don't forget to ask them.

Closing the interview & effective follow-up

A cliché in sales is "ABC – Always Be Closing" meaning you need to be focused on earning the sale from your customer. While an interview isn't directly analogous to a sales call, they are somewhat similar.

As an interviewee, you cannot just let the interview end without taking a few steps that ensure you'll get called back with either additional interviews or a job offer.

Here are a few tips to keep in mind as you come to the close of your interview:

Ask what the next steps are

You can add this to your list of questions. It's vital you know where they are in the process so you can set your expectation accordingly.

Be willing to ask "Do you see anything that would prevent me from moving forward?"

When you ask this, you may be presented with an opportunity to address any concerns they might have about you.

Always say "Thank You"

They didn't have to interview you, but they did- so at the very least say 'thank you' in person as you leave. Follow up with an email to each interviewer to thank them immediately after the close of your meeting. Want to go even further? Send a written thank you in addition to the email. Gratitude is not just the foundation of all virtue, expressing it is a dying art, and doing so will help you stand out.

Never ask about salary, benefits, or other compensation unless they bring it up.

Avoid this part of the conversation until an offer has been made.

You never waste time interviewing

All interviews are not just about gaining experience in how to interview; they expand your network. Even if you don't get the job you will have laid the foundation for future networking and potential openings down the line.

Don't focus on 'staircase moments'

The French word is 'l'esprit d'escalier' or 'staircase mind' and we've all had this happen to us. That moment when you say to yourself "Oh, I should have said *blank*!" Don't sweat what you said or didn't say – just move on and remember you did your best at the moment.

Ask about when you might hear from them

It cannot hurt to have a general idea to hear back from them about a decision since this will determine when you can follow up without seeming like a pest.

Cross your fingers

If you've done your best, don't lay awake at night worrying about if you said the right thing or if you'll get the job. Life is too short to waste it that way.

Appendices

"A mind that is stretched by new experiences can never go back to its old dimensions."

- Oliver Wendell Holmes, Jr

Appendix A: Resume Information Checklist

Your Resume Information Checklist

Employment History (Past and Present)

Start with your most recent position and go back 10-15 years.

    Organization:

    Title:

    Begin:

    End:

Key Accomplishments/Projects

Education Information

- Omit your high school education and any years of graduation
- Include Institution plus Degree or Coursework (if no degree)
- Including the focus of your study is optional if not relevant
- This section also includes training

Certification/License Information

    This can be included under Education

Volunteer and Community Involvement

Training

    This can be added to Education or as a separate section.

Technical Skills / Platforms

Awards and Honors

Things an employer should know about you

Industry Keywords

Appendix B: Sample Resume

Fun fact: 'Lorem ipsum' was developed as a dummy text sometime in the 20th century and has served as filler text by writers and publishers ever since then.

It is used here for illustration purposes of what text on a resume might look like.

First Name Last Name
(XXX) 555.1212 no_reply@domaindotcom

SUMMARY
Lorem ipsum dolor sit amet, consectetur adipiscing elit. Nunc malesuada tempus luctus. Proin facilisis erat a leo rhoncus ornare. Maecenas vehicula nunc dui, ac rutrum est posuere eget. Quisque molestie est sed vestibulum pulvinar. Vestibulum congue blandit purus, vel porttitor mauris malesuada quis.

- Mauris commodo et sapien ut dictum. Vivamus non arcu quam. Proin pharetra ultricies urna, molestie porta magna porttitor eu. Suspendisse ipsum quam, tincidunt et enim at, tristique laoreet lectus.
- Curabitur ac nisi congue, egestas diam eget, tempor lacus. Quisque vel varius ex. Curabitur ut risus erat. Vivamus a tortor aliquet, sollicitudin enim et, pulvinar nunc. Aenean pulvinar odio malesuada, pellentesque lectus et, euismod lacus.
- Lorem ipsum dolor sit amet, consectetuer adipiscing elit

EXPERIENCE
Position - Company   **Start Date - Present**
Mauris commodo et sapien ut dictum. Vivamus non arcu quam. Proin pharetra ultricies urna, molestie porta magna porttitor eu.
- Suspendisse ipsum quam, tincidunt et enim at, tristique laoreet lectus.
- Curabitur ac nisi congue, egestas diam eget, tempor lacus.

Position - Company   **Start Date – End Date**
Mauris commodo et sapien ut dictum. Vivamus non arcu quam. Proin pharetra ultricies urna, molestie porta magna porttitor eu.
- Suspendisse ipsum quam, tincidunt et enim at, tristique laoreet lectus.
- Curabitur ac nisi congue, egestas diam eget, tempor lacus.

Position - Company   **Start Date – End Date**
Mauris commodo et sapien ut dictum. Vivamus non arcu quam. Proin pharetra ultricies urna, molestie porta magna porttitor eu.
- Suspendisse ipsum quam, tincidunt et enim at, tristique laoreet lectus.
- Curabitur ac nisi congue, egestas diam eget, tempor lacus.

Fake Namerson – Page 2

(317) 555.1212
no_reply@domaindotcom

EDUCATION

Master of Science, Leadership	Central State University
Bachelor of Arts, Business Marketing	Smalltown College

LICENSE

Registered Widget Engineer - License #8675309	National Widget Board

CERTIFICATIONS

Six Sigma Black Belt	XYZ Corporation

TRAINING

Microsoft SharePoint Server Administration	Contoso Training

VOLUNTER EXPERIENCE

Board of Directors – Anytown Animal Shelter
Volunteer – Wheresburg Red Cross
PTA Member – Harper Valley School Corp.

Appendix C: Cover Letter Sample

Replace anything in [brackets] with the relevant information.

[Your Name]
[Phone]
[Email]

[Month xx, Year

[Hiring Manager Name]
[Hiring Manager Title]
[Hiring Manager Company]

Dear [INSERT HIRING MANAGER NAME HERE]

I would like to express my interest in [INSERT COMPANY NAME HERE] and the position of [INSERT POSITION TITLE HERE]. As a [SELF DESCRIPTION] I am known for [SAMPLE ATTRIBUTE THAT COMMUNICATES YOUR VALUE AS A CANDIDATE}. Below I have outlined how my skills match your requirements for this position. I appreciate your consideration for employment with [INSERT COMPANY NAME HERE].

Your Requirement:
[LIST JOB REQUIREMENT HERE]
My Qualification:
[LIST QUALIFCATION THAT MATCHES JOB REQUIREMENT]
Your Requirement:
 [LIST JOB REQUIREMENT HERE]
My Qualification:
[LIST QUALIFCATION THAT MATCHES JOB REQUIREMENT]
Your Requirement:
[LIST JOB REQUIREMENT HERE]
My Qualification:
 [LIST QUALIFCATION THAT MATCHES JOB REQUIREMENT]

My resume is included for your review. Thank you for taking the time to review my credentials and experience.

Sincerely,

[Your Name]

Appendix D: Resume Action Words List

Please Note: Examples are all shown in the past tense, so be sure to use present tense when describing your current job

Analytical / Financial

Analyzed

Assessed

Determined

Devised

Diagnosed

Estimated

Evaluated

Examined

Forecasted

Formulated

Integrated

Negotiated

Prioritized

Projected

Researched

Communication Skills

Authored

Composed

Convinced

Drafted

Edited

Marketed

Persuaded

Presented

Promoted

Handling Change

Adapted

Adjusted

Converted

Tailored

Creativity

Designed

Developed

Engineered

Envisioned

Produced

Shaped

Taking Initiative

Achieved

Advanced

Built

Coordinated

Created

Demonstrated

Established

Expanded

Implemented

Initiated

Introduced

Launched

Mobilized

Modernized

Revamped

Revised

Spearheaded

Updated

Problem Solving

Customized

Generated

Identified

Revitalized

Reinforced

Streamlined

Strengthened

Transformed

Producing Results (with Metrics)

Grew

Improved

Increased

Reduced

Maximized

Minimized

Modified

Reduced

Sales

Captured

Converted

Earned

Won

Generated

Negotiated

Technology

Coded

Deployed

Installed

Launched

Programmed

Rewrote

Refined

Tested

Upgraded

Leadership

Assigned

Administered

Chaired

Coached

Directed

Empowered

Enabled

Management

Facilitated

Fostered

Guided

Led

Moderated

Monitored

Supervised

Trained

Organizational Ability

Arranged

Budgeted

Calculated

Centralized

Compiled

Consolidated

Organized

Planned

Teamwork/Collaboration

Assisted

Collaborated

Partnered

Contributed

Expedited

Served

About the Author

Jason Mutzfeld is the Co-Founder and Chief Career Coach at Merrfeld. Building on a long career in education and technology training, Jason believes that finding the truth inside each person will foster the courage and passion that drives growth. He has a Master of Science in Instructional Design and Technology from Purdue University as well as training from The Second City and Disney Institute.

About Merrfeld Career Management

Merrfeld is a Career Management agency located in Indianapolis, Indiana offering coaching, resume services, and training to clients throughout the United States.

www.ingramcontent.com/pod-product-compliance
Lightning Source LLC
Chambersburg PA
CBHW071528040426
42452CB00008B/933